FAR FROM PARADISE

G000164687

An Introduction to Caribbean Development

James Ferguson

First published in Great Britain in 1990 by
Latin America Bureau (Research and Action) Ltd,
1 Amwell Street, London EC1R 1UL

©James Ferguson

British Library Cataloguing in Publication Data
Ferguson, James, *1956-*
    Far from paradise : an introduction to Caribbean development.
    1. Caribbean region. Economic development, ca 1960-1975
    I. Title
    330.9729

    ISBN 0-906156-54-8

Editor: Duncan Green
Design: Andy Dark/Art Depot, 18 Ashwin St., London E8 3DL

Drawings: Sergio Navarro pp.2,6,20,25,30,34,41,43,53,55

Photographs and graphics:
    Philip Wolmuth pp.4, 22/3, 25, 26(r), 28, 29, 31, 32, 34, 39(l), 40, 41(r), 42, 43(l), 44(l), 45, 53, 54, 55, 56, 57(r), 60
    West India Committee pp.5, 6, 9, 10, 11, 12(t), 13, 17, 23(r), 24, 26(l), 30, 33, 37, 41(l), 43, 44(t), 46, 47(t), 52, 57(l)
    The Mansell Collection pp.7(r), 10, 11, 12, 13, 14(t), 21(t), 22
    Jamaica Information Service pp.20, 37(r), 38
    Trinidad & Tobago High Commission pp.19, 49
    Oxfam pp.2, 3 Robert Wells, pp.27, 30(l), 36, 37(l)
    Belinda Coote
    Wellcome p.10
    Richard Hart p.16
    John Topham Library p.18
    Bernard Diederich p.51(t)
    Roshini Kempadoo/Format p.58

Cartoons: *Caribbean Contact* pp.27, 37, 48 *Caribbean Review* p.50

Cover photograph: Penny Tweedie/IMPACT

With thanks to Paul Osborn for researching additional materials and pictures

Typeset, printed and bound by Russell Press Ltd, Nottingham NG7 4ET

UK bookshop distribution by Central Books, 99 Wallis Road, London E9 5LN
Distribution in North America by Monthly Review Press, 122 West 27th Street, New York, NY 10001

Printed on straw-based paper

Contents

The Caribbean

UNITED STATES
OF AMERICA

Gulf of Mexico

Miami

BAHAMA ISLANDS

Nassau

ANDROS

CAICOS Is

TURKS Is

Atlantic Ocean

Havana

CUBA

MEXICO

GRAND CAYMAN

JAMAICA

Kingston

Greater Antilles

DOMINICAN
REPUBLIC

Port au Prince

HAITI

Santo
Domingo

PUERTO RICO

San Juan

VIRGIN Is

LEEWARD Is

ANGUILLA

ST MARTIN

BARBUDA

ST CROIX

ST KITTS

NEVIS

ANTIGUA

GUADELOUPE

MARIE GALANTE

MONTSERRAT

DOMINICA

Lesser Antilles

MARTINIQUE

ST LUCIA

Bridgetown

BARBADOS

WINDWARD Is

ST VINCENT

GRENADA

Port of Spain

TOBAGO

TRINIDAD

Belmopan

BELIZE

HONDURAS

Tegucigalpa

Caribbean Sea

CURAÇAO

BONAIRE

ARUBA

NICARAGUA

Managua

COSTA
RICA

PANAMA

Panama City

Cartagena

Caracas

VENEZUELA

GUYANA

SURINAM

CAYENNE

Georgetown

Paramaribo

Cayenne

San Jose

Pacific Ocean

COLOMBIA

Bogota

BRAZIL

0   100   200   300   400   500 miles

0   100 200 300 400 500 kilometres

Introduction

intasun

AR AND AWAY

ESCAPE TO DREAM LAND

...that the world is getting smaller and it's not difficult to see why. ...Intasun brings you still more of the world's most beautiful Far & Away places at remarkably low prices. ...imagination be captured by no less than five of Mexico's top resorts, with the widest choice of flights to suit you. ...der fabulous Jamaica with a selection of holidays bearing the ...mous Far and Away stamp of excellent value for money. ...ourse, this year we repeat the tremendous success of Thailand, ...and the Dominican Republic with a larger than ever range of superb beach hotels and resorts.

Intasun's "Lowest Price or Your Money Back Guarantee", our ...e to you of "Absolutely No Surcharges", and the high quality of ...vice – just sit back, relax and let us carry you Far and Away.

YOUR INTASUN HOLIDAY GUARANTEE

Living in Paradise

Nowhere in the world is quite as enchanting as the Caribbean.

Warm waters that run from deep blue to crystal clear turquoise.

Palm lined beaches of sugar white sand, baking in the sun all day and home to scurrying crabs at night.

Tropical islands ablaze with vibrant frangipani, bougainvillea and hibiscus.

Friendly bars and restaurants, drenched in the easy rhythms of calypso and reggae, where exotic rum cocktails are served up as easily as gin and tonics back home.

Sunrises that warm you down to your bones and sunsets that are unbelievably, impossibly romantic.

(Royal Caribbean Cruises brochure)

This is one image of the Caribbean, the image sold to thousands of would-be tourists each year as they dream of white beaches, blue sky and warm seas. The cliché is based on truth. The Caribbean is a beautiful region, where the scenery and climate combine to create a part of the world which to the visitor can seem like paradise.

But it is only a small part of the truth. What the tourist from Europe or North America experiences is far removed from everyday life for the great majority of Caribbean people. For most of the millions who live there, the region offers not just natural beauty but also great poverty. The market trader or 'higgler' who walks several miles to town in the hope of selling a few vegetables does not see her life as idyllic. Nor do the unemployed who are forced to live in the slums of the big cities. If asked, few factory workers or farm labourers would say they live in paradise.

The Caribbean, like other parts of the Third World, is a poor region. In each of its countries a small minority owns most of the wealth, while the majority of people are poor. One way to measure this poverty is to look at per capita Gross Domestic Product (GDP) — the average share of the wealth created in a country each year (see figure 1).

Although some things are the same price in the

Dream holidays....
that you can afford

Once, the exotic holiday worlds of the Caribbean and Mexico were just a dream for most people. Now Thomson have made that dream come true. Dominican Republic - brand new for Summer '90 - is deliciously Caribbean with a Spanish feel, Barbados is inviting and relaxed, lush Jamaica is beautiful and full of fun and exciting Acapulco is fashionable and international.

Relax on dazzling white beaches, enjoy blue skies and azure seas or try any number of sports on land or sea. And when evening comes, enjoy a cocktail as the sun goes down. Choose from a wide selection of value for money holidays in apartments or hotels and fly direct and in comfort, on modern wide-bodied aircraft, to the holiday spot of your dreams.

Florida

MEXICO

Acapulco

Jamaica

Dominican Republic

CARIBBEAN SEA

Barbados

Thomson CARIBBEAN CARNIVAL

Street scene in Port-au-Prince, the capital of Haiti

Caribbean as in Britain or the United States, most goods, especially those imported from abroad are much more expensive. There is little the majority of people in the Caribbean can afford to buy.

Not only do the people of the Caribbean earn less money than in Britain and the US. They also die younger, suffer more from preventable illnesses and many more of their children die in the cradle. A shortage of medical facilities — hospitals, doctors, medicines — is matched by a lack of educational opportunities. Many people in the region receive little or no schooling, and in some countries as many as 40 or 50 per cent of people cannot read or write. Housing, too, is a serious problem in the Caribbean.

Large numbers of people cannot afford decent homes, governments do not build enough new ones, and many live in slums or shacks, increasing the risk of disease.

Poverty and Wealth

Despite this poverty, however, the Caribbean has always been a source of great wealth. From the day Columbus set foot in what is now the Bahamas, the islands have produced valuable commodities such as gold, sugar, spices and oil, but they have not been used to the benefit of the majority. Instead, the Caribbean is a tragic example of how a region's

mi nevah have noh time
wen mi reach
fi si noh sunny beach
wen mi reach
jus people a live in shack
people livin back-to-back
mongst cackroach an rat
mongst dirt an dizeez
subjek to terrorist attack
political intrigue
kanstant grief
an noh sign af relief

o di grass
turn brown
soh many trees
cut doun
an di lan is ovahgrown

fram country to town
is jus thistle an tawn
inna di woun a di poor

is a miracle ow dem endure
di pain nite an day
di stench af decay
di glarin sights
di guarded affluence
di arrogant vices
cole eyes af kantemp
di mackin symbals af
independence

Linton Kwesi Johnson, *Reggae fi Dada*

wealth can actually make its people poor.

One reason is that the Caribbean's resources and the profits from them have often been taken out of the region. This began when the European nations first seized the Caribbean territories as colonies, and used them to produce sugar, tobacco, spices and other crops. These were exported to Europe and sold there, with most of the profits going to European merchants and governments. Ever since then, most of the Caribbean's exports have been controlled by US and European companies, which sold and kept the profits from them in their own countries. The Caribbean countries have only ever received a small proportion of the proceeds from the things they grow and make.

The governments of the region, whether before or after independence, have rarely managed to get a better deal for the commodities they export. On the one hand, Caribbean governments have often accepted that there is no alternative to the existing system of selling raw materials in the world market and that foreign involvement in their economies is necessary to create jobs and attract investment. How else could they sell their commodities, they argue, if they do not deal with large companies from other countries? On the other, it is always very difficult for small countries to challenge the companies with which they do business, since these companies can always look elsewhere for their suppliers. Through political choice and the pressures of the international trading system, the Caribbean countries have remained extremely dependent on outside interests for the export of their commodities.

Dependence and poverty are part of daily life in today's Caribbean. But this is not inevitable; it can be changed. In the recent past, governments in Jamaica and Grenada have tried to tackle these problems by reorganising their economies and changing their relationships with the outside world. Their goal was to achieve a different type of development for their countries. In each country, too, groups of ordinary people -farmers, traders, women — have come together to improve their own lives by trying different forms of development.

Development — For Whom, By Whom?

'Development' means different things to different people. In economic theory it generally means the process whereby a country moves away from agricultural towards industrial production as the basis for the economy. This process is supposed to bring benefits to the developing country. These include rising incomes and increased employment, as profits and jobs from industry replace the more uncertain business of growing food or crops for export. As more money enters the economy, so living standards should rise, giving people the opportunity to buy a wider range of goods. This creates a demand for more goods which, in turn, creates more employment as people are hired to produce them. At the same time, a developing country can spend money raised through taxes on vital areas such as health, education and housing. A developed country is industrialised and has sufficient schools, hospitals, houses, roads, etc to meet the needs of its population.

But not everybody shares this simple definition of development. Some would say, for instance, that

Figure 1	per capita GDP (US$/£)	Life expectancy	Infant mortality per 1000 live births
Haiti	360/ 225	52	123
Guyana	390/ 244	68	33
Dominican Republic	730/ 456	64	70
Jamaica	940/ 588	73	20
Trinidad	4200/ 2625	68	22
Barbados	5350/ 3344	72	11
Britain	10420/ 6512	75	10
US	18530/11512	75	11

Sources: World Bank 1989, UNICEF 1987

Market vendor in Roseau, Dominica

real development is not just about building up industry, but should be more concerned with improving the living standards of all sectors of society. Very often, industrial development fails to do this and simply benefits a small elite while changing the type of poverty experienced by the majority. In many developing countries, people from the countryside have flooded into the cities, hoping to find work in industrial centres. Some get jobs as low-paid factory workers; others are still unemployed. Neither group has gained much from this kind of 'unequal development'.

Another view of development stresses the importance of giving people, and particularly the poor, a greater say in the way their society is organised. All too often, decisions on development are not made by the people who have most to gain from social and economic change, but by those who already have power and influence. They often take decisions which favour their own interests, not those of the poor. The decision, for instance, to build a road or power station may appear to promise an improvement for all. But for those without access to transport or electricity, such an 'improvement' is often valueless. When talking about development, it is therefore important to ask the questions: development by whom and for whom? In other words, who stands to benefit?

This introduction to the Caribbean looks at the region's past and present through the perspective of development issues. It shows how the colonial period has left a lasting mark on the people and their daily lives. It also examines and evaluates the various measures which have been taken by governments to modernise and diversify their countries' economies and the role played by foreign companies and governments. By looking at four Caribbean countries' recent history — Jamaica, Grenada, Trinidad and Haiti — it emphasises the variety of the region's recent experiences as well as the common problems faced.

Grenada

First of all, our revolution is an attempt to build a new socio-economic development model. It is an attempt to solve our problems by new methods. It is the boldest attempt, in the history of the English-speaking Caribbean, to tackle the dire problems of underdevelopment which so drastically affect the lives of the mass of people in our region: the problems of poverty, illiteracy and poor education, substandard nutrition, unemployment, and all the other evils.

Maurice Bishop, Prime Minister of Grenada, 1981

The Roots of Underdevelopment

Serious study of the economic history of the Third World which is most vividly illustrated in the Caribbean, must begin with an understanding of three facts. There never was any attempt to produce what was needed but only to produce what someone else needed. Trade did not involve a calculated exchange involving surpluses but the importation of virtually everything that was needed and the export of virtually everything that was produced. Finally, the surplus which a group normally uses to increase its production was largely exported in the form of profit to the centre of colonial power. Hence, at every single level of importance, the natural economic process was diverted, thwarted, frustrated and ultimately destroyed. These propositions need restating not because they are original, but because they are basic to any understanding of the contemporary issues of Caribbean politics.

Michael Manley, *Jamaica: Struggle in the Periphery.*

1. Pirates and Plantations

Before Europeans arrived in the Caribbean, the region contained a group of more or less 'undeveloped' societies. The islands were inhabited by two main peoples, the Arawaks and the Caribs. Both groups had originated from the continent of South America, and as the Caribs gradually moved northwards from the mainland, invading each island in turn, so the Arawaks retreated ahead of them. Both societies had subsistence economies; they depended upon hunting, fishing and food gathering, and grew only a few crops for their own consumption. Private property was more or less unknown in these societies. Land and food were communally shared within small village settlements on the coasts, while people travelled from one island to another in canoes.

We have not harmed any of them... true, when they have been reassured and lost their fear, they are so naive and so free with their possessions that no one who has not witnessed them would believe it. When you ask for something they have, they never say no. To the contrary, they offer to share with anyone...

Hans Koning, *Columbus: His Enterprise*

Explorers and Colonists

These were the societies which the Italian explorer, Christopher Columbus, encountered when his first expedition, financed by Spain, arrived in the region in 1492. The 'discovery' was really an accident. Columbus was in fact attempting to reach India, which was already known to the seafaring European nations, and because he thought that he had found a westerly route to the Indian continent, he called the Caribbean the 'West Indies'. Profit was the driving force behind the expedition. Spain wanted to open up a new trading route to India, since the old routes through the Mediterranean had been disrupted by the wars of the Crusades and were controlled by the powerful city states of Venice and Genoa.

Even if Columbus was unsure of where he was and what he had 'discovered', his expedition showed the considerable progress that had been made in 15th-century Europe. With advances in navigation and ship building, European explorers could sail thousands of miles in search of profitable trade. And in the countries of Europe, too, the economy was developing from a feudal and agricultural system to one which was based more on manufacturing and trading. European merchants were interested in buying raw materials and goods from other parts of the world which they could then sell in their own or other countries. Goods such as silk, spices and sugar became very valuable as the wealthy classes in European society acquired a taste

Contemporary engraving of Columbus' 1492 expedition

for these new luxuries. This was the beginning of the merchant economy which hungered for overseas exploration and trade.

For Spain, 1492 was a pivotal year. It was the year the recently unified Spanish crown, under Ferdinand and Isabella, drove out the last Moors from the city of Granada, reestablishing absolute Christian rule after a 500 year battle. The Church was now ready to turn its attention outwards, and it encouraged expeditions such as that led by Columbus, since it believed that European travellers should convert the non-European peoples whom they met to Christianity.

Gold

However, Columbus' first priority was not religion, but gold. As he wrote in a letter to his patrons, Ferdinand and Isabella, 'Gold is the most excellent, gold is treasure, and who has it can do whatever he likes in this world. With it, he can bring souls to Paradise...' Noticing that the Caribs and Arawaks wore gold jewellery, he claimed possession for Spain of those islands which he saw and began the process of plunder which destroyed the Caribbean's original societies. Gold meant little to the native inhabitants; to the Spanish it meant everything, and they forced the natives (whom they called 'Indians') to provide it for them. In the world's first gold-rush, open-cast mines were dug, the natives were enslaved and put to work, and ships containing the valuable metal sailed back to Spain.

Every man and women, every boy or girl of fourteen or older, in the province of Cibao (of the imaginary gold fields) had to collect gold for the Spaniards. As their measure, the Spaniards used those same miserable hawks' bells, the little trinkets they had given away so freely when they first came 'as if from heaven'. Every three months, every Indian had to bring to one of the forts a hawks' bell filled with gold dust. The chiefs had to bring in about ten times that amount. In the other provinces of Hispaniola, twenty-five pounds of spun cotton took the place of gold.

Spanish colonists oversee the Indians collecting gold

Copper tokens were manufactured, and when an Indian had brought his or her tribute to an armed post, he or she received such a token, stamped with the month, to be hung around the neck. With that they were safe for another three months while collecting more gold.

Whoever was caught without a token was killed by having his or her hands cut off...

Hans Koning, *Columbus: His Enterprise*

The gold quickly ran out. Soon the Spanish invaders began to look elsewhere for fresh supplies and moved on to the potentially rich lands of South and Central America. For the Caribs and Arawaks, it was already too late. In 1492 there had been perhaps 300,000 of them on the island of Hispaniola alone; by 1514 only an estimated 14,000 were left. Many had died fighting against the invaders, but the majority died from overwork in the Spanish mines or from diseases which the Europeans brought with them. Those colonisers who remained in the islands realised that the region could create riches in another way, that it could be used to grow crops such as tobacco for export back to Europe. In particular, they recognised that the Caribbean's tropical climate would suit sugar-cane which they introduced into the islands (see *The Greatest Gift*).

Pirates and Plantations

But first they had a problem to overcome. After the extermination of the native inhabitants, there were not enough workers or slaves to cultivate the sugar. At first the colonists brought contracted labourers from Europe to work in the plantations. They were poor people or prisoners, some of whom volunteered (others were kidnapped) and who hoped to obtain a small amount of land for themselves at the end of their contract. But they were insufficient for the big sugar plantations. Many also died because of poor food and conditions and from diseases such as yellow fever. The sugar producers looked for another source of labour, and now they decided to import slaves not from Europe, but from Africa.

Spain had been the first European nation to seize and colonise the Caribbean islands. As other European countries saw the wealth which Spain was extracting from the region they, too, began to move into the area. At first, British and French pirates or buccaneers preyed upon the Spanish ships as they sailed back to Europe. Later, the governments of these and other European countries sent armies to

Ann Bonny and Mary Read, convicted of piracy in Jamaica in 1720

Sir Walter Raleigh sacking a Spanish settlement in Trinidad, 1595

fight the Spanish colonists and took certain territories for themselves. When Britain defeated the Spanish Armada in 1588, it ended Spanish naval supremacy. Over the next century Britain took possession of Antigua, Barbados and Jamaica, while the French colonised Martinique, Guadeloupe and the western side of Hispaniola (or what is now Haiti). Gradually the Spanish monopoly in the Caribbean disappeared. Many of the islands subsequently changed hands as European nations struggled for domination in the region.

Slavery

By the beginning of the 18th century all the islands had something in common, whichever European country controlled them; they all imported and used slaves on their plantations. The enslavement of Africans was nothing new. From the middle ages onwards, European countries had been willing to capture or buy black slaves who were often provided by Arab or Portuguese traders. They considered this morally acceptable, since the Africans were not Christians and were therefore thought to be inferior. What was different about the Caribbean slave trade, however, was its sheer scale. In the course of the 17th, 18th and 19th centuries, the slavers abducted an estimated five million Africans from their countries and sold the survivors in the Caribbean colonies.

Companies were founded in Britain, France, Spain, Holland and Denmark to supply the

The Greatest Gift

On his second voyage, in 1493, together with livestock, vegetables, wheat, barley, vine and fruit trees, oranges, lemons, melons and other plants, Columbus included, on his stop at the Canary Islands, the greatest gift of the Old World to the New — the sugar cane.

The cane introduced by Columbus came to be known as the 'creole' variety. This remained the dominant variety until the introduction of the Otaheite cane in the middle of the eighteenth century. An enthusiastic description in 1518 described 'fields of sugar cane that are wonderful to see, the cane as thick as a man's wrist, and as tall as the height of two men of medium stature'.

Hispaniola became the cradle of the Caribbean sugar economy. In a memorandum for his Sovereigns on January 30, 1494, Columbus wrote enthusiastically of the future of the industry in Hispaniola, and compared it with that of Andalusia and Sicily...

The sugar industry spread from Hispaniola to Jamaica, Puerto Rico and Cuba. Its development was gradual but steady. By 1523 there were thirty *ingenios* (sugar mills) in Jamaica; five years later there were ten in Puerto Rico, producing approximately 170 long tons....Such was the importance of the industry that Las Casas could write: *'this island of Hispaniola contains 40 or 50 sugar ingenios, and could have 200, which are more valuable and advantageous to the human race than all the silver, gold and pearls of England'.*

Eric Williams,
From Columbus to Castro: The History of the Caribbean 1492-1969

[Cutting Sugar Cane.]

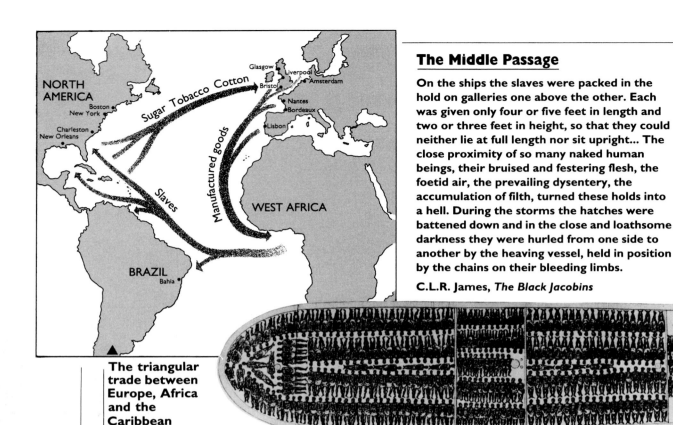

The triangular trade between Europe, Africa and the Caribbean

The Middle Passage

On the ships the slaves were packed in the hold on galleries one above the other. Each was given only four or five feet in length and two or three feet in height, so that they could neither lie at full length nor sit upright... The close proximity of so many naked human beings, their bruised and festering flesh, the foetid air, the prevailing dysentery, the accumulation of filth, turned these holds into a hell. During the storms the hatches were battened down and in the close and loathsome darkness they were hurled from one side to another by the heaving vessel, held in position by the chains on their bleeding limbs.

C.L.R. James, *The Black Jacobins*

Caribbean plantations with slave labour. In what was known as the 'triangular trade' ships set out from European ports such as Bristol, Bordeaux or Liverpool and sailed to the west coast of Africa. There, they bought slaves from local chieftains or other traders in exchange for manufactured goods such as weapons, metals or fabrics. The ships then crossed the Atlantic to the Caribbean, where they sold their human cargo to the plantation owners. In the final leg of the triangle, the ships then returned to Europe, carrying sugar and other tropical products for sale to European manufacturers. At each stage the traders made a large profit by exchanging one commodity (including the slaves) for another.

Slavery devastated Africa. Local and foreign traders looking for further victims tore apart the coastal areas with wars and raids, then went further inland in an effort to feed Europe's insatiable appetite for slaves. The great civilisations of West Africa slowly declined. Every year thousands of young men, women and children were stolen from their communities. For the slaves themselves, the experience was horrifying. Many died during the crossing from Africa to the Caribbean in overcrowded and filthy ships (see *The Middle Passage*). This crossing, known as the 'middle passage' (being the middle stage in the triangular trade), became notorious for its cruelty and death toll. Sometimes half or more of a ship's consignment of slaves died and were tossed overboard before reaching the Caribbean. The traders, however, made huge amounts of money from the business. Personal fortunes and the prosperity of cities like Bristol and Nantes were built on the trade in human beings.

Upon arrival in the Caribbean islands the slaves were sold according to their age, health and sex. Most were immediately put to work on the sugar plantations. They worked from dawn to dusk, planting or cutting cane. At night they slept in simple huts, provided by their owners, and on Sunday they were allowed to grow food on small plots of land. The slaves belonged to their masters and could be treated as they saw fit. Whipping, branding and other forms of physical punishment were commonplace (see *Pain and Pleasure*).

Some slaves escaped and formed free communities in the islands' more remote areas. These escaped slaves were called 'Maroons' (from the Spanish word, cimarrón, meaning wild) and defended themselves against recapture. In many cases the Maroons became a strong fighting force, and the colonists were forced to leave them in peace. Many other slaves, however, were unable to escape and quickly died. The colonists needed to replace them, and so the trade grew.

In contrast to the miserable existence of the slaves,

Pain and Pleasure

Punishment was a regular part of estate life and in the early days a planter could do much as he liked with his slaves. In time he came under stricter control as the laws relating to slaves were made less harsh, but the early slave code, as it was called, was very brutal. Punishment for what would now be regarded in most cases as minor offences ranged from death to the cutting off of an arm or leg, and terrible floggings. Revolt was treated as a most serious crime and punished accordingly. Running away from the plantations was a common practice, the penalty for which was also often severe. As late as 1830 — four years only before slavery ended — a slave woman called Congo Nancy was sentenced to life imprisonment at hard labour for escaping from Craig Mill estate in the old parish of St George and staying away for a period exceeding six months....

Opportunities for recreation were few, but these the slave learnt to make the most of. There were the Christmas and New Year holidays when the gay and colourful John Canoe (or Jonkonnu) bands roamed the streets, and the teams of pretty Set Girls dressed up in the rich clothes and jewellery of their mistresses, competed with one another in the lavishness of their costumes. There were the Easter Holidays which, being shorter, were called *pickney Christmas*; and the weekly carnival of the Sunday Markets, chief of which was that held in Kingston where, with noise and merriment amidst thousands of people, pigs, goats, fowls, yams and other vegetables were disposed of, as wells as such small home-made articles as mats, baskets, bark ropes, yabbas and jars; and delicacies too, like strawberries grown in the high, cool St Andrew mountains, grapes and melons.

But apart from these, there were the gatherings at night, when work was over, outside the huts; the singing and the dancing, and the story telling — stories of Anancy the cunning spider-man; stories of gods and animals, of Africa and its many wonders; stories of longing and despair, and stories of hope.

Clinton Black,
History of Jamaica

the white plantation owners lived in luxury. Installed in their 'great houses', which dominated the plantations, they imported everything that they wanted from Europe. In a letter written in the 1830s, Lady Nugent, a British aristocrat gave a graphic account of the lives of the planters.

'I don't wonder at the fever the people suffer from here — such eating and drinking I never saw. Such loads of all sorts of high, rich and seasoned things, and really gallons of wine and mixed liquors as they drink. I observed some of the party, today, eat of late breakfasts as if they had never eaten before — a dish of tea, another of coffee, a bumper of claret, another large one of hock-negus, then Madeira, sangaree, hot and cold meat, stews and fries, hot and cold fish pickled and plain, peppers, ginger

Slaves dancing during the Easter Holiday

sweetmeats, acid fruits, sweet jellies — in short, it was as astonishing as it was disgusting.'

Many planned to return to their country of origin as soon as they had made enough money to afford a comfortable retirement. The slave owners and their white employees often took advantage of their power over the female slaves. From these relationships were born the coloured or brown-skinned people, known by the pejorative term *mulattoes*, who formed a third class between the white colonists and the black slaves.

To justify this system, the colonists and their European partners developed a series of racist ideas and arguments. These claimed that the Africans deserved to be slaves because of their supposed inferiority to the Europeans. Since the Africans, they argued, were uncivilised and un-Christian; it was reasonable to enslave them as a means of converting them to Christianity. In fact, this argument was in direct contradiction with Christian ideas and teachings. They also suggested — although few people could have believed them — that the slaves were happier in the Caribbean than in Africa, since they were fed and housed by their owners. But above all, they argued that slaves were essential to the colonial economy; without them, the colonists asked, who would produce the sugar?

Europe's Sweet Tooth

Sugar, the 'white gold', brought riches to the Caribbean planters and industrialists who refined and sold it in Europe. The colonies became vital to the economies of the European countries, since they provided raw materials which could not be found in Europe and because they, in turn, bought manufactured goods back from the European producers. The colonial system was based upon a two-way trade. But many colonists resented the system, in particular the monopoly which the European governments held over their colonies. A Jamaican sugar producer, for example, had to sell to a British refiner, even if a Dutch refiner was prepared to pay more. Local producers began to rebel against such controls and to demand greater independence for the colonies. This was the beginning of Caribbean nationalism, the idea that the colonies should become self-governing nations.

The profits from sugar went partly to the planters themselves. Many left the islands and returned to Europe with their fortunes. They also went to European capitalists who refined and sold the sugar and who exported other goods to the Caribbean colonies. And governments, too, took their share of the profits through various forms of taxation. These huge profits helped to pay for Europe's economic development; it was sugar which largely financed Europe's Industrial Revolution. The great advances of the 18th and 19th centuries — the growth of factories and mass production, railways, ports and roads — were chiefly made possible by the colonial system and by the work of the slaves.

Despite the wealth it produced, the Caribbean itself remained extremely poor. The planters were interested in sugar alone. They prevented other crops being grown, as they would have taken up valuable space in the plantations. Food was imported into the islands and the development of other forms of agriculture was ignored. Schools were never built; the planters did not consider it necessary or wise to educate the slaves, while the colonists'

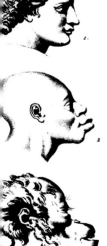

A 19th-century view of racial differences

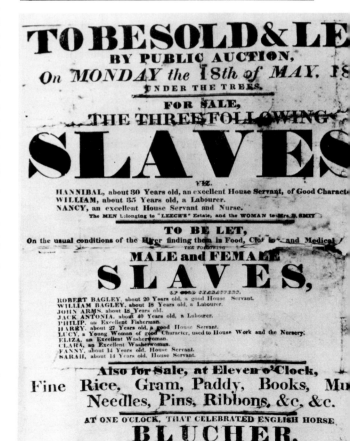

Not a Nail, Not a Horseshoe

The colonial system placed particular emphasis on the prohibition of colonial manufactures. In British North America copper smelting was prohibited in 1722, the manufacture of hats in 1732, and the Colonial Manufactures Prohibition Act of 1750 sternly forbade the manufacture of bar or pig iron, and provided for the abolition of colonial slitting-mills, tilt-hammers, and iron furnaces. Not a nail, not a horseshoe said Chatham, was to be manufactured.

Towards this end, the British Government discouraged the growth of towns in the colonies. In 1714 the English Customs agreed to the creation of additional ports of entry on the northern coast of Jamaica, provided that the inhabitants were not thereby encouraged to reside in the towns and set up manufactures for their own needs. Such a step, said the Commissioners of Customs, would discourage British trade and would distract the inhabitants of the colony from planting and raising sugar, which was more to the benefit of England.

Eric Williams, *From Columbus to Castro*

Inside a sugar factory

Cane is sweet sweat slain;
cane is labour, unrecognized, lost
and unrecovered;
sugar is the sweet swollen pain
*   of the years;*
sugar is slavery's immoveable
*   stain;*
cane is water lying down,
and water standing up.
Cane is a slaver;
cane is bitter,
very bitter,
in the sweet blood of life.

Faustin Charles, *Sugar Cane*

The social pyramid of the plantation system

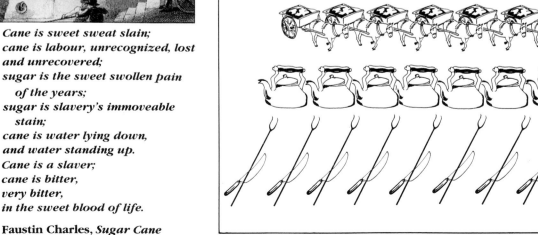

Governors
Planters
Attorneys
Managers

Overseers
Bookkeepers
Tradesmen

Poor whites

Free blacks
Mulattos

Domestic slaves
Skilled slaves

Field slaves

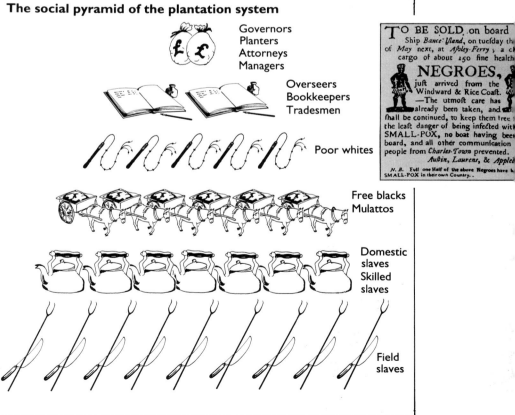

TO BE SOLD on board
Ship *Bance-Ifland*, on tuefday th
of *May* next, at *Afhley-Ferry*; a c
cargo of about 150 fine health

NEGROES,

juft arrived from the
Windward & Rice Coaft.
—The utmoft care has
already been taken, and
fhall be continued, to keep them free
the leaft danger of being infected wit
SMALL-POX, no boat having bee
board, and all other communication
people from *Charles-Town* prevented.
Aufiin, Laurens, & Applel

N. B. Full one Half of the above Negroes have
SMALL-POX in their own Country.

children were sent to Europe for their education. European governments often banned or blocked manufacturing, as they wanted the colonies to buy products from them (see *Not a Nail, Not a Horseshoe*). The islands were expected to produce sugar, to send it to Europe and to do little else. While Europe's governments and merchants grew steadily richer and Europe progressed, the Caribbean islands stagnated.

From the beginning of colonialism, outside needs and profits dictated the Caribbean's development. Just as the islands' gold had been shipped away to Spain, so the wealth created by sugar production sailed off across the Atlantic to Britain or France. Apart from the planters themselves (and many of them lived in Europe, leaving managers to run their estates), nobody in the islands, and least of all the slaves, benefited from the wealth and development which sugar could have provided. The plantations took only the most fertile land in the islands, leaving large areas idle. The planters shipped in some technology such as machinery for crushing the cane, but otherwise they never introduced modern techniques. The planters treated the islands as temporary homes, and felt no need to improve working conditions for their slaves. The system had gone as far as it could.

The Decline of Sugar: the End of Slavery

By the beginning of the 19th century sugar production had passed its peak. The colonies were producing too much and prices dropped. Not only were they competing among themselves and with other colonies such as Portuguese-controlled Brazil, but they were now also confronted with the danger of competition from Europe itself. Another form of sugar production had been discovered which used not cane, but sugar beet. This could be grown and produced in Europe. The colonial economies consequently declined. At the same time, a movement was growing in Europe for the abolition of the slave trade, arguing that slavery was morally unacceptable and could not be tolerated by the Christian societies of Europe.

Powerful though these arguments were, they were perhaps less important than the economic grounds for abolishing slavery. Many Europeans had realised that slavery was not only inhumane, but also fundamentally inefficient. They felt it would be less expensive to pay wages to free labourers than to keep them as slaves, because then planters would not have to feed and house their workforce. They also believed that labourers would work harder for wages than slaves, particularly if they were paid

Slave Revolts

From the introduction of slavery into the Caribbean at the beginning of the 16th century, the white planters and colonists lived in constant fear of slave revolts. Armed uprisings occurred frequently, particularly in the 18th century, when the slave population was at its highest. Revolts were crushed by the colonial militias, but this did not deter the slaves who had no other way of fighting for their freedom. The frequency of uprisings in the 18th century can be seen from this list of major revolts and the territories where they occurred:

1734 Jamaica
1736 Antigua
1737 Guadeloupe
1746 Jamaica
1752 Martinique
1760 Jamaica
1761 Nevis
1763 Suriname
1765 Jamaica
1769 Jamaica
1772 Surinam
1776 Jamaica; Montserrat

A peace treaty between Maroon fighters and the colonial authorities

The most famous slave revolt started in 1791 in the French colony of Saint Domingue. Led by Toussaint Louverture and later Jean-Jacques Dessalines, the slaves of Saint Domingue defeated the French army, a British invasion force and Spanish troops from the neighbouring colony of Santo Domingo. After thirteen years of war, Dessalines and his former slaves finally created the republic of Haiti in 1804 — the first independent black republic in the world and the result of the only successful slave revolution in history.

Spanish Town, Jamaica, on Emancipation Day, 1838

according to the amount they produced. This made good sense to many of the plantation owners, especially since new slaves were becoming increasingly expensive and difficult to obtain. And abolition, they thought, would also reduce the risk of slave rebellions against them (slave revolts were a very common event in the Caribbean — see *Slave Revolts*).

For various economic and humanitarian reasons, the European powers began to move towards ending slavery in their colonies. Firstly, the slave trade itself was banned, hence preventing the arrival of further Africans in the colonies even though slave traders broke the law and continued their business. Then, after much discussion and delay, the system of slavery was abolished, in 1833 in the British colonies, and in 1848 in those ruled by France. In Britain's territories alone an estimated 540,000 slaves were set free over a five-year period; for each of these the planters were paid compensation by the British government.

The first instinct of many freed slaves was understandably to get away from the plantations. Some managed to settle on small patches of land with which they could feed themselves. Others, however, stayed on to work as wage labourers in the sugar-cane fields, especially in islands where there was little available free land. The overall result was another labour shortage. As before, the planters looked for a way to import workers, and as before they opted for a system of contract labour. But this time they were not poor Europeans, but Indians and Chinese who came to work in the Caribbean on five or ten year contracts. Between 1838 and 1917 about half a million came to the region, replacing those former slaves who had left the plantations. The large sugar-producing territories of Guyana and Trinidad received most Indian labourers, and today these countries have as many people of Indian descent as of African.

'Bitter Cane'

At first the new system of wage labour proved more profitable than slaves. Productivity increased, and sugar continued to flow in huge quantities to Europe. In 1895 the British Caribbean colonies exported almost 25% more sugar than they had in 1828. Trinidad's sugar exports quadrupled during that period, thanks largely to the arrival of 99,000 Indian labourers. Gradually some British colonies such as Jamaica and Trinidad began to produce other crops and materials for export, while others, like Barbados and St Vincent, grew almost nothing but sugar. Here, the planters were unwilling to introduce new methods and technology, and they slowly fell behind other larger islands in the Caribbean such as

A modern-day Christmas procession in Spanish Town relives the slaves' traditional celebrations

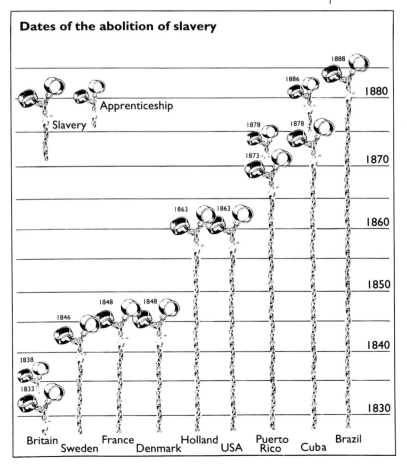

Dates of the abolition of slavery

Slaves in Barbados celebrate the arrival of emancipation

Cuba and Puerto Rico which were rapidly modernising their sugar industries. The British colonies were old-fashioned; they did not have the railways or big factories which other producers had built to increase their output. This was largely because they were still tied to Britain which now no longer required as much sugar from the Caribbean and did not want to pay for modernisation. On the non-British islands, on the other hand, in Cuba, Puerto Rico and the Dominican Republic, money from US investors and companies was paying for new equipment and technology which enabled these countries to increase their sugar exports, which enjoyed protected access to the US market.

By the 1930s the Caribbean colonies were no longer so important as a source of wealth, despite a temporary boom in sugar prices in the preceding decade. The islands had thousands of acres of sugar-cane, which by now nobody really wanted to buy, but no industries to produce the goods which local people wanted. Because they had always exported a single crop they had failed to develop other sorts of large-scale agriculture which would have helped them to diversify their production. Their development had been geared towards other nations' needs, not their own, and now the colonial powers no longer needed them. The Caribbean was left with hundreds of declining sugar plantations and a sick, under-educated, hungry people crammed together in plantation huts or urban shanty towns. This was the price the Caribbean had paid for its sugar.

Further Reading
Eric Williams, *From Columbus to Castro: The History of the Caribbean 1492-1969*, London, Andre Deutsch, 1983.
JR Ward, *Poverty and Progress in the Caribbean 1800-1960*, London. Macmillan, 1985.

Chapter Summary
■ Before Columbus arrived, the Caribbean was inhabited by the Arawaks and Caribs.
■ Columbus came in search of gold and a trade route to Asia.
■ In their search for gold, the Spanish enslaved and finally exterminated the Caribbean's native peoples.
■ When the gold and native people ran out, the Spanish and other colonial powers like Britain and France turned to sugar and slavery.
■ Slave-grown sugar fuelled the Industrial Revolution in Europe, but kept the Caribbean poor.

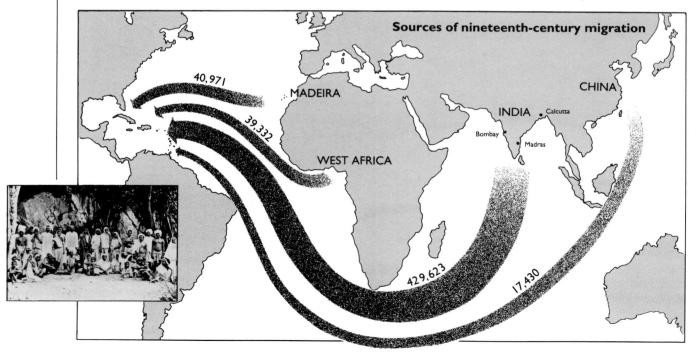

Sources of nineteenth-century migration

40,971

39,332

MADEIRA

CHINA

INDIA · Calcutta

Bombay ·

· Madras

WEST AFRICA

429,623

17,430

2. From John Bull to Uncle Sam

Poverty and Protest

In the 1930s, a hundred years after the abolition of slavery in the European-ruled Caribbean territories, conditions for the mass of people had not really improved. Nearly all the region's poor people were either subsistence farmers, growing barely enough food to feed their families, or were wage labourers in the plantations. Many were both, since sugar cultivation is a highly seasonal job, and so they would work on the plantations at harvest times and on their own smallholdings the rest of the year. Most squatted on the fringes of the big estates or on 'Crown Lands' that belonged to the colonial government but were usually unused and unproductive. Wages were extremely low; some visitors were amazed that families could survive on so small an income — many barely managed it. Few could afford to eat a balanced diet, and social facilities such as schools and hospitals were utterly inadequate.

At Orange Bay the Commissioners saw people living in huts the walls of which were bamboo knitted together as closely as human hands were capable; the ceilings were made from dry crisp coconut branches which shifted their position with every wind. The floor measured 8 feet by 6 feet. The hut was 5 feet high ... In this hut lived nine people, a man, his wife, and seven children. They had no water and no latrine. There were two beds. The parents slept in one, and as many of the children as could hold on in the other. The rest used the floor.

The situation became even worse as the collapse of the international banking and trading system, known as the Depression, led to a drastic fall in world commodity prices. Many of the Caribbean territories were almost entirely dependent upon sugar as their principal export. Now, as its value on the world market plunged, the plantations sacked their workers and poverty spread. These plantations were no longer always owned by individual planters as they had been during the 18th and 19th centuries. Many had been taken over by foreign companies such as the British-owned Tate and Lyle which employed large numbers of workers in their fields and factories. Because of their wealth and power, these companies could buy up the best and most fertile land in any area, forcing smallholders and independent farmers into the less fertile regions of the islands. Much of the rest of the best land was owned by absentee landlords, and often left uncultivated.

Tension built up between the poor smallholders and the large plantation owners, between the wage labourers and the foreign-owned companies, provoking regular uprisings in the islands. In 1937 and 1938, for instance, there were many strikes and protests in Jamaica and Trinidad as the poor desperately attempted to defend themselves against worsening living conditions. In all, 47 people died, 400 were injured, and canefields and estate buildings were burned in a series of disturbances throughout the region. In some areas the authorities declared martial law and sent in the troops to restore order (see *The Kingston Riots*).

Many people joined trade unions during this period, bringing together not only agricultural workers but others such as dockers and transport workers. Another symptom of the deepening crisis and the people's response was the growth of nationalism. A kind of nationalism first existed among the plantation owners in the preceding two centuries because this class resented the monopoly of trade which the European governments forced upon the colonies. Now, however, it was the poor

Cartoon from around 1910 portrays President Theodore Roosevelt and his "Big Stick" of American military intervention. The U.S. invaded independent countries of the Caribbean dozens of times during the gunboat diplomacy years.

The Kingston Riots

From an early hour mobs began to collect and parade the streets of Kingston. They rapidly became mischievous. Dust bins were overturned and their contents scattered on the streets; some Chinese shops and bakeries were attacked and goods and money stolen...

As time passed the mobs were much increased by men and women who might have gone to work if left to themselves, but were either intimidated from doing so by the mob or were unable to withstand the attraction of having a day out. They continued to parade the streets and began to threaten shopkeepers with violence unless they closed their shops and released their assistants; as a result all shops in the centre of the city had to close.

Disorder then became general and the police were insufficient in numbers to control the situation. Persons of all classes going to business were set upon, public property was destroyed, streets blocked and tramcars attacked.

Extract from the British Government report on the general strike and rioting in Jamaica in May 1938.

Pro-independence demonstration in Jamaica

of the towns and countryside who began to think that independence from the European powers and their economic domination would improve their lives.

A further response to the region's poverty and racism lay in the search for African roots and identity among sections of the black community. Jamaican-born Marcus Garvey emerged as a charismatic spokesman for the black people of the Caribbean and elsewhere, and his United Negro Improvement Association linked groups in the US, Africa, Europe and the Caribbean. Garvey was feared and detested by the colonial authorities, while his natural supporters — the poor black majority — were forbidden to vote in elections. As such, Garvey's political career ended in failure, but his message — 'Africa for the Africans, those at home and those

abroad' — had, and still has, a powerful impact throughout the Caribbean.

The Second World War further disrupted the already weak Caribbean economies, although there was no fighting in the Caribbean itself. The Atlantic trading routes to Europe were blocked by hostilities and ships were frequently attacked, while the European nations could no longer afford to import non-essential goods such as sugar or bananas. Cut off from their traditional markets, the islands could not even import the goods which they needed from Europe. Economic conditions worsened and hardship increased. In 1945 the findings of the Moyne Commission, an investigative body sent to the British Caribbean territories by the Colonial Office in London, were published. The report outlined the extent of the region's problems: little local industry, unplanned agriculture, inadequate education and health facilities, poor housing and widespread unemployment (see *The Moyne Report*).

Despite this dismal picture, the Moyne Commission did not suggest that the region should develop its own industries to escape from having to import the most basic necessities from abroad. Instead, it proposed that the existing system should be reformed. Agriculture should be modernised, but should still be directed towards export crops. Social welfare and the infrastructure should also be improved. But according to the Commission, the way to achieve these aims was not by developing the region's resources for domestic use, but by attracting foreign aid and investment and by exporting abroad. In short, the Colonial Office proposed that the British colonies in the Caribbean should continue to depend upon foreign interests rather than work towards self-sufficiency.

The Moyne report is a fascinating document, not only because it describes social conditions in the

The Moyne Report

It is not an exaggeration to say that in the poorest parts of most towns and in many of the country districts a majority of the houses is largely made of rusty corrugated iron and unsound boarding...sanitation in any form and water supply are unknown in such premises, and in many cases no light can enter when the door is closed. These decrepit homes, more often than not, are seriously overcrowded, and it is not surprising that some of them are dirty and verminous in spite of the praiseworthy efforts of the inhabitants to keep them clean. In short, every condition that tends to produce disease is here to be found in a serious form.

Moyne Commission Report, 1945.

Loading grapefruit for export, Trinidad

Caribbean in a very detailed and accurate way, but also because it shows how colonial attitudes towards the region had evolved. By 1945 the Colonial Office in London clearly thought that territories such as Jamaica and Trinidad had outlived their usefulness. Britain had valued and defended its Caribbean colonies for as long as they were profitable, but now that they were in decline it seemingly had little help to offer. Rather than proposing real changes, it merely suggested ways of reforming the same system.

Migration

Discouraged by this lack of development, many people decided to leave. From the last years of the 19th century thousands had moved from island to island within the region in search of work. The Panama canal which was built between 1881 and 1914 employed some 83,000 workers, mostly from the English-speaking Caribbean. The conditions were appalling; over 25,000 workers died in the course of the canal's construction from disease and

Emigration to the UK

'Sometimes I look back on all the years I spend in Brit'n', Moses say, 'and I surprise that so many years gone by. Looking at things in general, life really hard for the boys in London. This is a lonely miserable city, if it was that we didn't get together now and then to talk about things back home, we would suffer like hell. Here is not like home where you have friends all about. In the beginning you would think that is a good thing, that nobody minding your business, but after a while you want to get in company, you want to go to somebody house and eat a meal, you want to go on excursion to the sea, you want to go and play football and cricket. Nobody in London does really accept you. They tolerate you, yes, but you can't go in their house and eat or sit down and talk. It ain't have no sort of family life for us here.'

Sam Selvon, *The Lonely Londoners*.

Go To ENGLAND THROUGH UNIVERSAL

ON ANY OF THE DATES

• M/V FRANCESCO MOROSINI ... SE
• S/S AURIGA .... SEP
• M/V SANTA MARIA .... OC
• M/V ANDREA GRITTI .... OC
• S/S NASSAU .... OC

UNIVERSAL TRAVEL SERVICE
TOWER STREET KGN DIAL

SHIPPING AND AIR SERVICE

EMBARKATION NOTICE
THE M.S.
"ANDREA GRITTI"
will sail from KINGSTON
THURSDAY, OCT. 6th.
— Baggage not required during the voy
MUST BE DELIVERED to the Baggage Ma
at NO. 1 PIER
between the hours of
8.00 a.m. & 3.00 p.m.
TODAY — WEDNESDAY 5th.
— Embarkation will commence at 8 a.m.
Thursday, Oct. 6th, and ship will depart in
afternoon. Lunch will be served on board to
passengers embarked.

The *Ascania* arrives in Southampton with 1,000 immigrants from the Caribbean, April 1961

'There were adverts everywhere: "Come to the mother country! The mother country needs you!" That's how I learned the opportunity was here. I felt stronger loyalty towards England. There was more emphasis there than loyalty to your own island... It was really the mother country and being away from home wouldn't be that terrible because you would belong.'

'I went to Peak Freans that used to have loads of part-time jobs and this woman said to me "We've got jobs, yes, but we can't give it to all your people". I was surprised but I didn't take it as racist then... I thought it was reasonable for her to say that.'

'One of the things that shocked me was looking around and seeing English people doing manual work. It seemed so depressing the picture that I built up in my mind. It wasn't that I thought it was the golden land but the streets, the space, the houses all capped together and no spaces and chimneys. It seemed very dull.'

'We took the train from Plymouth to Victoria Station. It was night when we came there. It was cold... the first thing I noticed, I look on all the houses and I say what a lot of factories.'

'It was because other people were coming to England and I understand that they were doing good. They sent for relatives and things like that; they could buy a home, they're doing well. There wasn't any employment in Jamaica... some people could find their way out but some people, if they hadn't got a proper start, they could not survive, so I came.'

Elyse Dodgson, *Motherland*

Emigrants as percentage of West Indian Populations

	†Population from 1960 census	‡Total emigration to UK 1955-61	Emigrants as % of population
Jamaica	1,609,814	148,369	9.2
Barbados	232,085	18,741	8.1
Trinidad & Tobago	825,700	9,610	1.2
British Guiana	558,769	7,141	1.3
Leewards	122,920	16,025	13.0
Antigua	54,060	4,687	8.7
Montserrat	12,167	3,835	31.5
St Kitts-Nevis-Anguilla	56,693	7,503	13.2
Windwards	314,995	27,154	8.6
Dominica	59,479	7,915	13.3
Grenada	88,617	7,663	8.6
St Lucia	86,194	7,291	8.5
St Vincent	80,705	4,285	5.3

†provisional figures   ‡Jamaica 1953-61, M.S.D.

accidents. The expanding sugar and banana industries in Cuba, the Dominican Republic and Central America also attracted many West Indians from the British and French colonies who hoped to escape poverty at home. Between 1951 and 1960 over 200,000 people from the Caribbean migrated to the US; many never returned. Major cities such as New York and Miami now have large, permanent populations of people who originate from the Caribbean. Major communities include those from Cuba, Haiti, Puerto Rico, the Dominican Republic and Jamaica.

Britain, too, seemed to offer the hope of employment and a new life, and thousands from the British colonies went there to do low-paid jobs in hospitals and transport. They were welcomed by the British government which needed workers to build up the country's industries and social services after the Second World War. Between 1960 and 1962 alone, an estimated 168,000 people left for Britain and most decided to stay there. This mass migration acted as a safety valve in the colonies, reducing the number of unemployed. Yet it also took from the Caribbean many workers, skilled and unskilled, who might otherwise have contributed to the region's development. Life was not always easy for those West Indians who came to Britain. They often suffered prejudice and discrimination, bad housing and poor wages (see *Emigration to the UK*).

The Independence Movement

Trinidadian sailors march in independence ceremony

Gradually the movement towards independence gathered momentum. Some territories had already gained their independence (Haiti in 1804, the Dominican Republic in 1844, Cuba in 1898), while in others, such as the French colonies of Martinique and Guadeloupe, the colonial power and most people in the islands were against the idea. Instead of independence, in 1946 Martinique, Guadeloupe and Cayenne voted to be 'overseas departments' of France, with theoretically equal rights to the rest of

France. Several Dutch colonies also agreed to remain tied to Holland, although Aruba is meant to achieve independence in 1996.

In the larger British territories, however, the majority of people wanted full independence, as they wished to break free from the system of colonial dependence and choose their own national leaders and policies. But the independence movement and their political parties were not always led by representatives of the poor majority even if many had originated in the trade union and labour movement. Instead, many of the leaders were from the small local middle or upper classes, who had been educated and trained within the colonial system. Some had been to British universities, built up successful businesses or careers and prospered under colonialism. Along the way, this regional elite had absorbed many colonialist ideas and values. Among these was the belief that the Caribbean territories, even when officially independent, should remain linked economically and politically to their European rulers and to other major powers. Others, however, favoured a more decisive break from these colonial ties and argued that the Caribbean territories should be truly independent.

The people of the Caribbean had little experience of real democracy or independence. Since the 18th century, the European colonies had been allowed a limited amount of self-government. Councils had been elected in order to organise local administration, but the electors were only those people who had a certain income or paid a certain amount of tax. In other words, democracy was reserved for the small class of white planters and administrators who controlled the colonies. In Jamaica in 1863, for instance, only 1,798 people out of a population of 441,264 were entitled to vote! Slowly more people were enfranchised and the powers of the councils were increased. But the colonial authority (in Britain's case, the Houses of Parliament) still controlled all decisions in the areas of defence and foreign policy. Even after universal suffrage had been introduced in the 1940s and local political parties were contesting elections, the colonies were still really administered from the Colonial Office in Whitehall. What most people wanted was complete independence and the chance to vote for their own parties and policies, free from British control.

They finally won that right in the 1960s and 1970s, when the great majority of British colonies became politically independent states. Jamaica and Trinidad gained independence in 1962, Guyana in 1963, and Barbados in 1966. Others followed later: Grenada in 1974, Dominica in 1978, St Lucia and St Vincent in 1979. As the Union Jack was lowered over these territories and new national flags were raised, the

The British flag is lowered in Jamaica, 1962

Princess Margaret with Norman Manley (left), Premier of Jamaica, 1958

people of the newly independent nations were optimistic about the future. Now they had the opportunity to choose for themselves what sort of development would best suit their needs. In theory, at least, they were now in charge.

Yet how real was this independence? The new nations were supposedly able to choose their own governments, draw up their own policies and trade with whichever countries they wished. But in reality their options were limited. They could either remain formally tied to Britain (and many recognised this by joining the British Commonwealth) or they could look to the US for trade and investment within their economies.

Their choices were limited because the independent Caribbean countries were mostly very small in area and population and were therefore unable to compete on equal terms with the larger, industrialised countries within the world economy. Neither did many have big enough populations to support industries which would produce goods for the domestic market. They were also still extremely underdeveloped, having been used for three centuries merely as suppliers of cheap commodities to Europe. Having always produced little else but sugar for European consumption, the islands had none of the machinery or expertise which they needed in order to start producing essential items for themselves. So it was obvious that they would have to import such things from abroad and pay for them with hard currency (US dollars) from locally produced exports. From the outset the new Caribbean nations were dependent both upon more powerful foreign countries and upon their own traditional exports. They could not become self-

sufficient overnight, but many economic experts insisted that they should start working towards a greater degree of economic independence.

The leaders of the independent countries may have talked about such goals, but in fact they did little to achieve them once they were in power. The habits of colonial dependency were hard to break, and it would have been impossible to change the Caribbean countries' traditional economic activities immediately. But many of the new political leaders had done well from the old system and saw no reason to introduce too many reforms. Instead, they explained that the best policy was to continue with existing forms of production and trade, so that money could be earned from exports to other countries. In particular, they recommended that the Caribbean nations should strengthen their links with the major foreign powers.

The US and its 'Backyard'

The major foreign power was, of course, the United States. After the Second World War it had become the most powerful industrial country in the world, overtaking the European nations. The US, too, had once been a colony (it had been divided among several European powers) and had won its independence in 1783 after war with Britain. Since then it had opposed European colonialism in the Western Hemisphere. Because of its geographical proximity the US gradually came to view the Caribbean as its 'backyard'; an area which it, and not the European countries, was entitled to control.

This control took two related forms. Firstly, there was economic control by US companies and corporations, which invested in the Caribbean countries' economies and took their profits back home to the US. Secondly, there was political and military control by the US government; the US supported governments of which it approved and acted against those of which it disapproved. Approval or disapproval depended on those governments' attitudes towards US companies and their investments.

The US replaced Britain as the major outside influence in countries such as Jamaica, Trinidad and

US troops take control of Santiago, Cuba, 1898

Barbados. Although they remained members of the British Commonwealth, they became increasingly dependent upon the US for trade and financial aid. Britain accepted this change in the region's political climate. During the Second World War, for instance, it had given the US permission to build military bases in six of its Caribbean colonies in exchange for 50 out-of-date warships. Now, although it was still politically and economically important in the Caribbean, Britain saw itself overtaken by the US. The US also dominated other territories including Puerto Rico (invaded and colonised in 1898), the US Virgin Islands (bought from Denmark in 1917 for US$25 million), the Dominican Republic and Cuba.

The main priority for successive US administrations was to keep the Caribbean politically 'stable'. This meant that the US was unwilling to allow governments to appear which did not share its own political system. During the 19th and 20th centuries the US had often used 'gunboat diplomacy', invading other countries when it disapproved of their governments and policies (see *The Big Stick*. More recently, however, in 1959, a

The Big Stick

Between 1900 and 1950, the US invaded or occupied countries within the Caribbean Basin 17 times. These countries included Cuba, Honduras, Panama, Nicaragua, Haiti and the Dominican Republic. Most of these invasions were meant to protect US investments or to safeguard strategic interests such as the Panama Canal which opened under US control in 1914. Later, however, US interventions became more openly political. In 1954 the US supported a military coup in Guatemala which ended the moderate reforms of Jacobo Arbenz's government. Arbenz had planned to hand over nearly 500,000 acres of unused land, owned by the US company United Fruit, to landless peasants.

In 1965 the US sent 20,000 Marines to the Dominican Republic in order to prevent an insurrection from restoring democratically-elected Juan Bosch to power after he had been ousted by a military coup. Bosch had refused to sell off state-owned sugar plantations and industries to private companies and US investors. Perhaps the most famous case of US intervention took place in 1961, when the CIA organised a force of 1,400 mercenaries to invade Cuba. When the troops landed at the Bay of Pigs they hoped that Cubans would rise up to overthrow Fidel Castro's communist government. In fact, the Cuban people fought against the US-backed

mercenaries and drove them out of the island within two days.

The pattern of US intervention has continued into the 1990s. In December 1989 over 20,000 US troops invaded Panama in order to overthrow General Manuel Noriega, accused by the US government of involvement in the cocaine trade. For many years previously, however, Noriega had been treated as a loyal ally of the US and was on the CIA's payroll when George Bush was its director.

US cavalrymen in the Dominican Republic, 1916

successful revolution in Cuba had thrown out a corrupt dictatorship despite US backing. Led by Fidel Castro, the Cuban revolution had then nationalised US-owned industries (although it had compensated the owners) and declared Cuba a communist country. US administrations subsequently treated Cuba as a threat to their own national security, claiming that a communist country in the Caribbean was likely to foment revolution in other countries in the region. After Cuba, the US tried even harder to keep the former British colonies politically friendly.

Part of the US invasion force in Cuba, 1898

The other major interest of the US was economic. It realised that the recently independent countries of the Caribbean were economically weak and that they would want to attract foreign trade and investment. For many US companies this was an obvious way to increase business and profits. Not only did the Caribbean countries need products which they could not manufacture for themselves (cars and televisions, for example), but they also had resources of their own which could be exploited. Gradually US companies began to move into the Caribbean, selling their products and buying crops and raw materials in exchange. Often, however, they did not merely buy these materials; they also began to extract them for themselves, paying the Caribbean governments for the right to do so.

Economic and political concerns came together in the US view of the Caribbean's geo-political significance. During periods of East-West tension US policy makers feared that small Caribbean countries could fall prey to Soviet influence or that Cuba could act as a local base for subversive activity against US economic interests. In particular, the US feared that political instability could affect the lucrative functioning of the Panama Canal as well as endangering supplies of oil which pass through

The traditional and the modern: fishing in Dominica and car production in Trinidad

THE YANKEES BACK

Well, the day of slavery back again!
Ah hope it ain't reach in Port of Spain.
Since the Yankees come back over here
They buy out the whole of Point-a-Pierre.
Money start to pass, people start to bawl,
Point-a-Pierre sell, the workmen and all.
* Fifty cents a head for Grenadians,*
* A dollar a head for Trinidadians;*
* Tobagonians free, whether big or small;*
* But they say, they ain't want Barbadians*
* at all.*

(from The Mighty Sparrow)

the Caribbean on their way from the Middle East to transhipment points and refineries in the region.

A New Beginning?

The independence won by the Caribbean nations was far from complete. Although they were, in theory, in control of their own development, they had to contend with a powerful neighbour and its hostility towards communism, or anything it regarded as such, within its own 'backyard'. At the same time, the US was the home of companies which wanted to control the way the Caribbean nations developed their economies. Because these economies had always been geared towards exporting a few commodities and importing most other goods, they were extremely dependent upon foreign markets and suppliers. Political independence was therefore no guarantee of economic independence. Long-standing independent nations such as Haiti, the Dominican Republic and pre-revolutionary Cuba knew this, since they remained almost exclusively reliant on the US for trade and investment.

The newly independent Caribbean states faced a dilemma. They could rely upon foreign countries and companies to provide their imports and market their exports; or they could attempt to develop and restructure their own economies by themselves. The first option was perhaps easier, but it meant that, as before independence, the profits from producing commodities were likely to be removed and exported overseas. The second option was altogether more difficult, since it involved starting up new industries from nothing, learning new skills and techniques and replacing imports with locally produced goods. At the same time, the Caribbean countries' population and spending power were too small to support large-scale domestic industries. In some cases it was obvious that the Caribbean nations would have to depend upon foreign imports. Specialised machinery and high technology products, for instance, would have to be bought from companies in the US or Europe. But it was possible to produce more basic and essential items without importing them, and thereby create jobs and diversify the economy.

Further Reading
Gordon K. Lewis, *The Growth of the Modern West Indies*,
London, Macgibbon & Kee, 1968.
Jenny Pearce, *Under the Eagle: US Intervention in Central
America and the Caribbean*, London, Latin America
Bureau, 1982.

Chapter Summary

■ The Great Depression of the 1930s further increased poverty in the Caribbean, leading to violent unrest and a rise in trade unionism and nationalism.

■ After the Second World War many people left the Caribbean for the US and Britain, searching for jobs, but often encountering prejudice and discrimination.

■ Most people in the English-speaking Caribbean wanted independence, however the leaders of the independence movement were often members of the local elite and were keen to maintain economic dependence on Europe and the US.

■ Political independence came in the 1960s and 1970s, but was undermined by continued economic dependence on foreign governments and companies and the traditional Caribbean system of exporting commodities in return for imports of manufactured goods and food.

■ After the Second World War the Caribbean became part of the US 'backyard', dominated by both US companies and its government.

■ The US government used force and economic power to reward allies and punish those who tried to choose an alternative road to development.

3. Paradise plc

Emerging from three centuries of colonialism, the independent Caribbean countries had to decide what path to development they wished to follow. This depended to a large extent upon what resources they had, how they planned to produce them, and to whom they wanted to sell them. Some of the countries were apparently more fortunate than others, as they had particular resources which were valuable in the international market. Oil had been discovered in Trinidad in 1907, while Jamaica, along with Haiti, Guyana, the Dominican Republic and Surinam, had been mining bauxite (the ore used for the production of aluminium) since the 1950s. Other countries did not possess these obvious advantages but had others. They had all-year-round warm climates which made them suitable for tourism, they had largely agricultural economies, based on fertile land, and they had large numbers of potential workers. All of these attracted foreign-based companies which were eager to do business with the newly independent Caribbean states.

The Transnationals

Since the Second World War the world's economy has been increasingly dominated by the activities of transnational corporations or TNCs. A TNC is a firm which produces its goods or services outside its country of origin and which operates in a number of foreign countries. Most well-known companies — Coca-Cola, Barclay's Bank, Ford, for example, — are TNCs or are part of larger TNCs. Companies such as these, which may be based in the US or Europe, not only export their goods and services around the world, but they also produce these goods in different countries. Why?

Electronics assembly plant, Antigua

* By setting up production plants abroad, the TNCs get easy access to the raw materials which they need and therefore avoid the trouble and expense of importing them to the US or Europe.
* They can pay their workers abroad much less than in their own countries.
* By moving into foreign countries, the TNCs are able to sell their products there, while at the same time sending their profits back to their headquarters.

Transnational corporations are usually based in rich, developed and industrialised nations such as the US, Japan and (to a lesser extent these days), Britain. Many of them are hugely wealthy organisations, employing thousands of workers and making vast profits. In 1987 Jamaica's Gross Domestic Product was US$2,860m, whereas the

UK banana company Fyffes signs an export agreement with the Jamaica Banana Board

largest multinational company, Unilever, had an annual turnover almost ten times greater. To continue making these profits TNCs endlessly search for fresh commercial opportunities all over the world. The developing countries are an obvious target, since they contain undeveloped resources and new markets for the TNCs' products. The mostly US-owned TNCs saw the recently independent Caribbean countries as a promising area for expansion.

Inviting Investment

Caribbean governments and business communities usually welcomed the TNCs, as they thought they would be able to share in the profits from the development of their economies. The governments hoped to tax the TNCs on their activities and profits, and businessmen looked forward to jobs as local agents or representatives of the TNCs. The governments encouraged the TNCs to exploit resources or to set up factories in the hope that employment would be created locally and that the TNCs would pay a fair price for the resources which they used. But the TNCs' main interest was not the welfare of the countries in which they wished to do business. Their first priority was making profits which they could then send back to the US or Europe. The interests of the poor people were by no means the same as those of the TNCs and their local agents.

Agriculture: The Fat of the Land

Agriculture was one existing area which the Caribbean governments wanted to develop and where TNCs quickly moved in. The British-based

Corporation	No of subsidiaries	Main Business
Canada		
Alcan	9	Mining
Bata	3	Shoes
France		
Club Méditerranée	8	Travel
Banque Nationale Paris	5	Banking
Switzerland		
Nestlé	13	Food
United Kingdom		
BAT Industries	6	Tobacco
Barclays	88	Banking
Booker McConnell	17	Agriculture
Cable and Wireless	13	Communications
Geest Industries	6	Agriculture
Tate and Lyle	9	Agriculture
UK/Netherlands		
Unilever	4	Food
Royal Dutch Shell	18	Oil
US		
Alcoa	8	Mining
Castle & Cooke	6	Agriculture
Chase Manhattan	11	Banking
Citicorp	18	Banking
Coca Cola	13	Bottling
Exxon	16	Oil
Holiday Inn	13	Travel
ITT	14	Communications
United Brands	9	Agriculture

Selected North American and European Corporations in the Caribbean, 1984

Source: *The Other Side of Paradise*

Cocoa in Grenada — destined for the UK

Banana production in Jamaica

PUNCHLINE by @CHRISTIAN

FATHER WHY IS IT THAT OUR PEOPLE AREN'T GETTING ENOUGH FOOD TO EAT?

I'M AFRAID THERE'S SOMETHING IN OUR FIELDS TODAY, MY SON ...

FATHER, WHAT IS IT?! DROUGHT?! LOCUSTS?! RATS?!

THAT HAS COMPLETELY WIPED OUT OUR TRADITIONAL HARVEST.

CASH CROPS...

companies, Tate and Lyle and Geest, had been producing and exporting sugar and bananas since before independence, and they remain dominant today. They were joined by US companies such as United Brands (known in Britain as Fyffes) and Gulf & Western which owned large plantations and which also bought crops from local producers. In many ways this system was not much different from that described in the Moyne Commission report of 1945. The large companies took their pick of all the best land, leaving the small farmers to scrape a living from the least fertile areas. The large plantations were modernised with the introduction of railways and machinery, but the smaller farms could not afford to introduce new techniques or machinery. The TNCs could dictate the prices which they would pay for bananas or other crops, and if the small farmers refused these prices, the TNCs could easily look elsewhere for other suppliers.

Agricultural production remained geared towards export and not towards local consumption. Bananas, sugar, citrus fruits, coconuts, cocoa, tobacco and spices were shipped to the US or Europe, while local people were unable to buy the basic foods which they needed. The Caribbean islands import basic foods from the US and elsewhere, and export 'exotic' foods such as pawpaws, mangoes, breadfruit, ackees and coconuts. There have been two serious consequences for the Caribbean's development. Firstly, the islands remain highly dependent upon foreign companies for the production and marketing of their own agricultural resources. Secondly, they are unable to feed themselves and are forced to import up to 50 per cent of their food. The Caribbean became a region producing what it does not consume and consuming what it does not produce. This means profits for the companies both from exports and imports at the expense of poor people

who cannot afford to buy even such basic foodstuffs as milk or flour.

Industry: Foreign Factories

Industrial development was another option. This strategy had clear advantages for the Caribbean countries. It would create jobs for local people and produce goods which until now had been imported from abroad. The experience of Puerto Rico in the 1950s and 1960s suggested that manufacturing could create dramatic economic growth and employment (see *The Puerto Rican Model*).

The Caribbean governments actively encouraged the TNCs to come in and set up local factories by offering to:

* waive tax on TNCs' profits for set periods of time after they began operations

* shield the TNCs from competition by blocking imports from their rivals overseas, effectively giving them a monopoly in the local market

The TNCs were naturally enticed by these concessions. Cheap labour was another attraction, since the TNCs can pay Caribbean workers much less than workers in their own countries to produce the same goods in their factories. According to one TNC assembly plant manager in St Kitts, quoted in *The Other Side of Paradise:*

'They work more minutes per hour at 10% higher labour productivity than in the United States, and at wages one-tenth those in the United States'.

The industries take two forms. There are those which produce goods — clothes, shoes, drinks etc — for local consumption. So Bata might open a shoe factory and retail network in Trinidad in order to make and sell its product in that country. But there are also those which are designed to produce goods not for local consumption, but for re-export to

The Puerto Rican Model

Starting in 1947, US corporations were invited to open factories in Puerto Rico with promises of a low-wage work force, freedom from US income taxes, and tax-free repatriation of profits. 'Operation Bootstrap', as it was called, was to build a modern industrial state on the ruins of Puerto Rico's stagnant sugar economy. Its deeper purpose was to bring the Island into the US economy as an industrial enclave supplying US firms with cheap labor.

Tax exemptions were one reason firms located in Puerto Rico. The other was the Island's special status as a US colony — not stated in so many words, but a reality nonetheless behind the title of 'freely associated state'. This relationship meant that firms could expect compliant local authorities and a stable poltical climate, while enjoying low wages typical of the Third World. It also meant US federal subsidies were available to build highways, port facilities and other infrastructure needed by investors.

Operation Bootstrap was touted as an economic miracle, and for a while, it appeared to be. Its results included:

■ Average economic growth of 6% in the 1950s, 5% in the 1960s, and 4% in the 1970s.
■ US capital investment increasing from US$1.4 billion in 1960 to US$24 billion in 1979.
■ Second highest per capita income in Latin America.
■ Literacy and life expectancy approaching that of the US.

■ Highest per capita level of imports from the US in the world, and 34% of total US direct investment in Latin America.

Behind these glowing figures, however, lay a different reality. Puerto Rico's rapid industrialization was accompanied not by rising employment, but by relentlessly rising *unemployment*. Official unemployment stood at around 12% in the mid-1960s; by 1975 it had risen to 20%, and this was considered an underestimation of true joblessness. Over this same period, and especially after 1970, Puerto Rico became heavily dependent on subsidies from the US federal budget. These subsidies, which stood at US$119 million per year in 1950, soared to US$3.1 billion per year in 1979.

Contrary to the self-reliance its name implied, the Bootstrap model made Puerto Rico dependent on foreign capital. This capital became increasingly mobile as the transnational corporations extended their operations around the globe. The result was an erosion of investment in Puerto Rico, and mounting dependence on US subsidies.

Catherine A. Sunshine,
*The Caribbean:
Survival, Struggle and
Sovereignty*

49 MAJOR COMPANIES HAVE PLANNED THEIR SUCCESS ALONG THE SAME LINES.

Puerto Rico's Caribbean Development Program is one of the most dynamic profit-generating initiatives in the Western Hemisphere. Or, for that matter, anywhere else in the world. And it's no wonder corporations such as Johnson & Johnson, Westinghouse Electric and Hanes Knitwear have become avid participants.

Puerto Rico, along with 22 of its Caribbean neighbors, now offers the best of all worlds to all kinds of businesses. By setting up a Complementary Production Project, your company gains multiple advantages. First, you benefit from the lower labor costs of most Caribbean countries. And secondly, you enjoy all the advantages Puerto Rico offers: 100% U.S. federal tax credits, 90% Puerto Rico tax exemption, highly skilled and educated work force (fully 98% of all plant managers in Puerto Rico are Puerto Ricans), ultra-modern communications systems, plus an extensive shipping and air cargo network for easy access to U.S. and overseas markets.

Find out more about this uniquely profitable program. Because now, more than ever, Puerto Rico is the gateway to new business opportunities for your company.

For a copy of our informative booklet, "Puerto Rico's Caribbean Development Program" write to Commonwealth of Puerto Rico, Economic Development Administration, Dept. WSJ 1024, 1290 Avenue of the Americas, New York, NY 10104 Or call 800-223-0699 (in New York State, 212-245-1200 Ext. 437)

PUERTO RICO
Profits are our biggest export.

Making parts for Ford and Chrysler, Dominican Republic

foreign markets. In these cases, the TNC often imports the materials into the Caribbean country, the goods are manufactured there, and the TNC then re-exports the finished products for sale in other countries. All that the Caribbean countries contribute is cheap labour. For example, a TNC might set up a clothing factory in Jamaica. Shirts or trousers are produced in the US and sent to Jamaica, where local workers simply stitch them together. The finished products are then sent back to the US and sold there.

This system has done well for the TNCs. By employing low-paid Caribbean workers, they have cut their costs and increased their profit margins. Its effect on the Caribbean's development has been less fortunate. On the one hand, it has created some employment, mostly among local women (who are paid even less than men). On the other, it has done nothing to encourage self-sufficiency and has even worsened certain problems. Many people, for instance, leave poor rural areas for the cities, hoping to find work in the factories. This causes the cities to expand too quickly, creating overcrowded slums. The governments modernise ports and roads, but merely to help the TNCs get their products to and

from the factories. And since the local governments pay for these improvements, they have less to spend on bettering conditions for people in other areas. The roads around industrial centres, for example, are often better than those used by small farmers in the countryside to take their produce to market.

Most seriously, the Caribbean people are forced to rely upon foreign businesses for employment and for the goods which they need. Almost everything is imported. The materials used in production, the technology and machinery, the managers of the factories nearly all come from abroad. At the end of the process both the finished goods and the profits disappear abroad, leaving few benefits for the Caribbean governments and their people. What the TNCs and their local agents have gained from the Caribbean enclaves, the majority of people have lost. Rather than producing goods for themselves, they are producing goods which are taken and sold abroad for profits which they do not share.

Tourism: Selling Sunshine

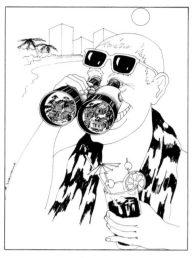

Punch Drunk

Every night the same songs are requested in the lounge of the British Colonial Sheraton in Nassau. The newly arrived, sunburned batch of tourists drink rum punches while listening to the standard Harry Belafonte rendition of the Caribbean banana-boat song 'Day-O' and popular calypso and reggae tunes. Outside the hustlers on the street 'pssst' passers by with whispered offers of 'ganja', 'white nose candy', and 'black pussy'. In St Lucia, amused little kids stand on the beach watching the terrace of the Couples resort where rows of visiting white women are learning to sway their hips as the natives do.

Tom Barry, Beth Wood and Deb Preusch, *The Other Side of Paradise*.

The third development strategy which the Caribbean governments attempted was building up a tourist industry. The region has a warm climate throughout the year and can offer sunshine and beautiful beaches to tourists from colder countries. These tourists from the US and Europe were expected to contribute to the economy by bringing dollars and pounds into the Caribbean and by spending them locally. Once again, the TNCs were heavily involved. Familiar names such as Trust House Forte, Sheraton and Holiday Inns now dominate Caribbean tourism, owning the majority of the region's hotels and resort facilities. These foreign companies soon took over the tourist industry and often benefited more from tourism than the countries in which they operated.

* The airlines which bring tourists to the Caribbean are chiefly owned by foreign companies which make their own profits and give nothing to the Caribbean countries.
* The hotels were mostly built by foreign construction companies and not by local contractors.
* Bookings for Caribbean holidays are usually made in the tourists' own countries; the money spent on holidays never even reaches the region.
* Once the tourists are in their hotels, they are normally offered imported food and drink, depriving local farmers and producers of a new market.

By these methods the TNCs have maximised their profits and minimised the role of local people in tourism.

Tourism has brought some benefits to local people. It has created some jobs, even if they are largely seasonal and poorly paid. Improvements

Majorettes welcome a cruise ship in Jamaica

have also been made to public services such as communications and transport for the benefit of the tourists, but these are useful to everybody. Local businesses such as craft shops and restaurants are also able to cash in on tourism. But these benefits are relatively limited, especially when weighed against the negative impact of tourism. This takes several forms; resentment against the luxurious lifestyles of wealthy foreigners, an increase in prostitution and begging, exploitation of local workers by foreign-owned hotel chains, and an artificial rise in the price of land. In some Caribbean countries, for instance, local people cannot even use their own beaches, which are reserved for foreign tourists. VS Naipaul, the Trinidadian writer, expresses the resentment towards tourism felt by many West Indians (see *Tourism: A New Slavery?*).

Many tourists in the Caribbean never actually stay on an island as such. These are the cruise ship tourists who travel from one country to another, sleeping and eating in the artificial atmosphere of their ship. On their brief excursions on dry land, they spend little money and receive only a superficial impression of the island's character. Nevertheless, in many Caribbean ports the days on which cruise ships arrive are ones of great activity by small traders and hopeful guides.

Tourism is especially vulnerable to foreign arm-twisting, because bad publicity about a particular country can easily deter potential holiday makers. Haiti's tourist industry collapsed completely in the mid-1980s when the country was inaccurately blamed for the AIDS epidemic. The US, in particular, is capable of ruining a Caribbean country's tourist industry by discouraging its citizens from travelling there on political grounds, and did precisely that when one Caribbean country, Grenada, decided to pursue an independent course of development (see p.40).

Banking: Dodging the Taxman

Caribbean governments also encouraged banks and other financial institutions to come to the region. To make it worth their while, some Caribbean governments agreed not to tax the financial TNCs on their transactions (in other countries they had to pay tax on each item of business). In return, the banks were expected to provide employment and to pay the governments for the right to do business

Tourism: A New Slavery?

These islands were small, poor and overpopulated. Once, because of their wealth, a people had been enslaved; now, because of their beauty, a people were being dispossessed. Land values had risen steeply; in some islands peasant farmers could no longer afford to buy land; and emigration to the unwelcoming slums of London, Birmingham and half a dozen other English cities was increasing. Every poor country accepts tourism as an unavoidable degradation. None has gone as far as some of these West Indian islands, which, in the name of tourism, are selling themselves into a new slavery.

**VS Naipaul,
The Middle Passage.**

Hotel workers on strike in Tobago

Repainting an oil storage tank, Trinidad

in their countries. In the countries where this took place — the Bahamas, Bermuda and the Cayman Islands — the governments have in fact received relatively little revenue and almost no employment has been created. The banks were not really doing business there; instead they acted as 'offshore' banks, merely transferring funds (often only on paper) through their Caribbean offices as a tax dodge. This operation needs little more than a telephone and a telex machine, so few jobs have been created. Once again the Caribbean has gained little, while offshore banking has boosted profits for foreign corporations. Another problem has been the presence of 'money-laundering' firms in the Caribbean which act as a means of recycling dollars made from the drug trade and other criminal activity.

Several scandals in the late 1980s revealed that millions of dollars pass through bogus banks in the region as a result of the cocaine industry.

A more recent trend is the introduction of service industries based on new technology. In Jamaica and Barbados particularly, large numbers of workers are employed in the processing of data for US firms, often meaning little more than hours at computer screens, inputting zip codes for mailing lists. This data is sent back to the US by satellite or cable, enabling the companies to pay Caribbean (and mostly women) workers lower wages than they would have to pay in the US.

Buried Treasure: Oil and Bauxite

Nature had blessed two English-speaking Caribbean countries with huge mineral wealth: Jamaica with bauxite and Trinidad with oil. These two commodities are extremely valuable and offered the countries' governments the hope of freeing their people from underdevelopment. Oil refining and bauxite mining require a large amount of capital investment in machinery and transportation, so the governments of Trinidad and Jamaica were faced

Confidence is built on a solid foundation. And Trinidad and Tobago is that foundation.

A solid citizenry, a stable political system, a skilled labour force, a fertile land replete with mineral resources have combined to make the Republic one of the soundest foundations on which to build a future.

Scotiabank is cognisant of the nation's potential. That is why we are confident of and committed to Trinidad and Tobago.

With a strategic network of 18 branches, a well trained and motivated staff and our international connections, we are the right bank to deal with when doing business in Trinidad and Tobago.

Join in our confidence

Scotiabank 🌀
Strength .Integrity .Service

Foreign-owned banks dominate the skylines of Caribbean cities

with a choice. They could either try to set up nationally-owned companies to produce and export these commodities, or they could invite TNCs to take over this work in exchange for payments on the commodities produced.

Oil in Trinidad

When Trinidad became independent in 1962 its oil industry had been dominated for half a century by British Petroleum and Shell. The TNCs' profits were beginning to fall, however, and in 1968 and 1974 respectively they sold their interests at a good price to the government of Trinidad. Rather than keep the former BP concerns as a nationalised industry, the government then sold them to another TNC, Tesoro Petroleum of Texas. The former Shell section did remain nationalised, but other TNCs, notably Amoco and Texaco, control much more of Trinidad's oil production than does the government. This means, of course, that decisions about investment and development are not taken in Trinidad, but in the US headquarters of the TNCs (see *Company Islands*). And while these companies pay the Trinidadian government for the oil which they export from the country, they also make large profits which are exported to their own countries of origin. The Trinidad oil workers have consistently demanded the nationalisation of the US-owned TNCs, claiming that the companies are likely to pull out of Trinidad if their profits drop.

Bauxite in Jamaica

Jamaica's experience with bauxite has been broadly similar, although it has not received the short-lived windfall which oil brought Trinidad. Bauxite mining began in 1952. After independence, the Jamaican government invited the TNCs to come in and produce and export bauxite, believing that the country could not afford to set up its own industry. These companies agreed to pay the government a certain sum for each ton which they exported. They shipped the ore out of Jamaica to be processed into aluminium in the US, where it was then used in the manufacture of cans for food and drink, machinery and military equipment. The TNCs paid the Jamaican government a very low price for the unrefined bauxite which amounted to about two per cent of the much higher price of finished aluminium. When the Jamaican government tried to change this system, it led to friction with the TNCs (see p.36).

Especially when the Caribbean countries own valuable natural resources, they are likely to be exploited by the powerful TNCs. Trinidad, it is true, has received significant wealth from its oil deposits and many thousands of Trinidadians are employed in the industry. Yet, these positive factors must be weighed against the fact that about 80 per cent of the country's economy is controlled by foreign interests and that planning of economic development is out of the government's hands. The drop in world oil prices from mid 1982 onwards undermined Trinidad's economy still further.

Jamaica's problems are even more serious. Relatively few Jamaicans (approximately 2 per cent of the national workforce) are employed in bauxite mining, and the value of this commodity dropped significantly until a revival in the late 1980s. As a result, the TNCs may lower their payments or stop their operations altogether, as they have in other Caribbean countries such as Haiti.

Whose Profits?

Every one of these development strategies, whether in agriculture, industry, banking and new

Open-cast bauxite mine at Mandeville, Jamaica

Company Islands

In 1965 the following statement by Texaco's Chairman of the Board, who was on his third visit to Trinidad, appeared in a full page paid ad in the Trinidad *Guardian*:

'Texaco has projected its...expenditures for this calendar year at more than US$600m...Where will Texaco spend this sum of money? Quite naturally, the people of Trinidad, just as the people in some other areas where we operate, would be interested in knowing if some of this money will be invested in their home area. The answer to this question [depends on] the economic conditions and stability of the country being considered for such investment and how these compare with other countries competing for such investment.

I would like to say that we are very proud of our record here...We sincerely hope that nothing will come up in the future to mar this record'.

technology or the exploitation of natural resources, has strengthened the power and influence of the TNCs within the region and increased its dependence upon them. TNCs make large profits which they do not reinvest in the Caribbean's future, but send home to companies and shareholders in the US or in other developed countries. It is true that these relationships with the TNCs have benefited some local people. Some have found jobs in the new industries, and governments have received revenue from the taxes on exports of their national resources. But the Caribbean has lost more than it has gained. The islands have wasted their chance to plan their own development and have handed over economic control to outside organisations more concerned with their own profits than with the wellbeing of the Caribbean people.

Many people argue that the Caribbean governments had little choice in this respect, that they could not afford to do without the powerful TNCs or establish new industries on their own. But others believe that the governments should not have given away so much control over their economies and that the TNCs' domination of the region should be limited. This second attitude became more widespread after the first decade of independence, when it became increasingly obvious that genuine economic development could not be left in the hands of the TNCs. During the 1970s some Caribbean governments tried to change the existing system in order to increase their economic and political independence and improve the living standards of the poor majority.

Further Reading

Tom Barry, Beth Wood and Deb Preusch, *The Other Side of Paradise: Foreign Control in the Caribbean*, New York, Grove Press, 1984.

Chapter Summary

■ As part of their expansion after the Second World War, a number of US and European TNCs moved into the Caribbean.

■ Caribbean governments and business classes welcomed them, hoping for increased revenue from taxes and jobs.

■ TNCs operate in agriculture, manufacturing, tourism, banking and finance and mineral extraction (chiefly oil in Trinidad and bauxite in Jamaica).

■ In each case TNC influence has grown over the years, but local people have obtained few of the expected benefits. In many eyes, TNCs became a barrier to development, since they took their profits overseas and made the Caribbean increasingly dependent and vulnerable to foreign control.

4. Hard Decisions

By the 1970s different Caribbean nations had tried various development strategies. Some had worked better than others, but none had really solved the problem of domination by big business or improved the lives of their poorest people. In response, political parties and movements sprang up in the Caribbean countries, challenging existing development strategies and offering radical new approaches. In the 1970s and 1980s two countries had governments which sought new paths to development: Jamaica and Grenada. What did these governments seek to achieve and what problems did they encounter, notably from the US? How do these experiments compare with the experience of Trinidad, a third English-speaking nation which has followed a more conventional development model?

In contrast, Haiti is a country that has had no progressive development strategy since its independence in 1804. Neither has it experienced any of the reforms or social improvements that have taken place elsewhere in the region. Instead, it has a long history of military rule and dictatorship, as well as extreme poverty and inequality. The fall of the Duvalier dictatorship in February 1986 seemed to promise a new beginning, but subsequent events have dashed such hopes.

Jamaica's 'Third Path'

Before and after independence in 1962, the Jamaican economy had expanded based on bauxite and its flourishing tourist industry, which had both replaced agriculture and particularly sugar as major earners of foreign currency. By 1970, however, the country was in serious trouble. Unemployment was up from 13 per cent in 1962 to 24 per cent in 1972; the 1962 Commonwealth Immigration Act had stopped emigration to Britain; wages were falling and prices rising; and large sectors of the Jamaican economy were in the hands of foreign TNCs. People, and especially the poor majority, were eager for change, and in 1972 the People's National Party (PNP), led by Michael Manley, won a general election.

The PNP promised a 'third path' for Jamaica. This meant rejecting both dependency on foreign companies and Cuban-style communism. Jamaica was to be economically and politically independent, tied neither to capitalism nor communism, but choosing a middle way which would respond to the needs of the people. The PNP government made a series of changes to the structure of the economy:

* It nationalised parts of the sugar industry, textile businesses, flour mills, and some banks and compensated their owners. The government ploughed their profits back into the national economy.

* The government increased the tax on the TNCs' bauxite exports. Within two years, the sum received from the TNCs had jumped from US$22 million to US$170 million per year.

* The PNP wanted to form an International Bauxite Association, bringing together all bauxite-

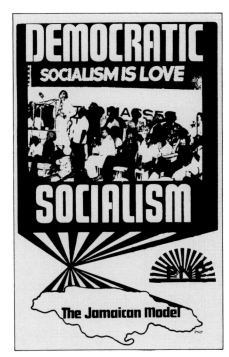

PNP leaflet from the 1970s

producing countries, so that they could negotiate as a united group for fairer prices from the TNCs.

* The government started a programme of land reform which bought up areas of land from TNCs and private landlords, and handed them over to local farmers and cooperatives.

Such measures genuinely benefited the Jamaican people, even if a small rich minority resented what they saw as an attack on their privileges. The power and influence of this minority was out of proportion to its numbers, and some of its members managed to disrupt the country's economic changes. They spirited large amounts of capital out of Jamaica and invested it in US banks and industries. Many business owners and managers left the country, creating a serious shortage of skilled personnel. The rich minority felt threatened by the PNP's proposed reforms and by Manley's talk of socialism.

Despite these setbacks, living and working conditions improved for the majority. Manley introduced minimum wages and set hours in many workplaces, started sickness benefits and maternity leave and made advances in education and health. House building programmes were undertaken, and special schemes for reducing youth unemployment were introduced. Above all, a larger share of profits, which before had disappeared abroad, remained in the country and were used to pay for these sorts of social development. The government also wished to increase the people's say in decision-making, believing that occasional general elections did not, in themselves, amount to a genuine democracy. As a result, community councils were formed, which dealt with local issues and problems.

US Opposition

This 'third path' was understandably popular with most Jamaicans, who at last felt they had a government which cared about them. But the US response was very different. Washington suspected that the PNP was leading Jamaica towards communism. In particular, because Michael Manley insisted on developing closer ties with Cuba (in US eyes, a sign of disloyalty), the US administration began to show its disapproval. It drastically reduced aid to Jamaica, encouraged US companies to withdraw their investment, and Jamaica's share of the world bauxite market fell, as TNCs looked elsewhere for cheaper supplies. All this amounted to a US embargo against Jamaica, simply because the country had chosen to develop in a way which the US thought ran counter to its regional interests. And these were not the only measures which the US used in order to destabilise the PNP government. Washington launched a propaganda offensive both inside Jamaica and in the US, painting the island as violent and politically unstable, thereby discouraging tourists and businesses from going there. US tourist arrivals in Jamaica dropped by almost a quarter between 1974 and 1976, despite having risen dramatically since the 1960s. US car manufacturers also blamed the Manley government

Agricultural cooperative established by the PNP government

Anti-IMF riot in Jamaica, 1985

Michael Manley

for higher bauxite prices, while increasing the price of cars for US consumers. In fact, despite the rise in the bauxite tax, the four main US alumininium companies made profits of over US$250m in 1976.

Jamaica was obviously not a communist country. Its economy was largely in private hands, the government had been elected by a popular vote, and opposition parties and newspapers were allowed to operate freely. But these facts did not prevent the US from treating it as 'communist' and attacking its alternative approach to development. As US aid and investment gradually dried up, the island's economy became weaker. Jamaica was producing less and could not afford to pay for necessary imports such as oil and food. Its balance of payments deteriorated, as the money it made from exports and tourism could not keep up with the money it spent on imports; it went badly into debt. It had to find sources of hard currency and was forced into the arms of the International Monetary Fund (IMF), an international banking organisation dominated by the US.

The IMF agreed to lend money to the Jamaican government, but only if it reversed its development policies and adopted austerity measures that would cut government spending. The government at first resisted but eventually had no choice, and was forced to abandon the development strategy which had briefly promised to transform the lives of the majority of Jamaicans. In return for vital loans, the government reluctantly cut wages, reduced government spending on education and health and brought in new taxes. Bus fares, for example, increased by 50 per cent, while basic foods also went up. Meanwhile, the PNP's opponents in Jamaica continued their campaign against Manley's reform programme, leading to open conflict and widespread political violence.

In 1980 disillusioned Jamaicans voted the PNP out of office, to be replaced by the conservative Jamaica Labour Party (JLP), led by Edward Seaga. The IMF had succeeded in its aims, having undermined an

Kingston market scene

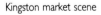

Edward Seaga

Life Under Seaga

The following are extracts from interviews with women attending an advice centre in Kingston. They are not isolated cases, but are typical of the situation experienced by thousands of women and children in Jamaica today.

Veronica lives in Kingston suburb with her two small children aged four and seven and her grandmother who is blind and housebound. They live in one room for which they pay J$60 (£10) a quarter. The room has no electricity and the nearest water supply is in the next door house. She has a part time job making bags, for which she is paid J$25 (£4.16) a week. Her elder child attends the local school whilst the four-year old is cared for by his great grandmother.

Veronica is the eldest of five children. Her four brothers and sisters are still of school age and living with their aunt in another part of town. She has no contact with the father of her children and receives no financial support for her family.

'Friends feed the children sometimes. We can't manage on my earnings. I have to pay the lease on the room or we would lose it, then where would we go? We eat mostly rice and calaloo (a type of spinach). I used to buy chicken necks and backs for the children, but we can't afford that any more. Prices just go up and up. It frightens me to think what will happen. Starve to death I suppose.'

Sandra lives on her own with her two children aged six and seven months. When she first met the father of her children he was working on a building site. 'We were happy for the first few years, then he lost his job and we had to make do on my earnings. I used to sell fried fish and bammy (a type of cassava cake) in the market, but the fish got too expensive and no one could afford to buy it so I had to give that up. We had nothing then but a boy to support and another on the way. It was too much for him. He left and I haven't heard from him since.'

Sandra supports her two children by begging on the streets. 'When I have to go out to get food I leave the baby with the boy. I have to keep him off school but what else can I do? Sometimes I send him out to find scraps on the street with the other kids. It's the only way'.

Oxfam, *A Case Study of Jamaica*, 1985, Belinda Coote

experiment in development which the US found unacceptable.

The JLP immediately returned Jamaica to the old strategy, obtaining renewed TNC investment and reestablishing close political links with the US. Washington restored and increased its aid (US$200 million in 1981 and 1982) and the embargo stopped. Yet even so, after 1980 the JLP did little to improve conditions in the country. Jamaica's debt to foreign banks has doubled since 1980, while unemployment increased still further. In 1979 it cost almost the whole of one legal minimum wage to feed a family of five, but by 1985 the same amount of food cost two and a half times the minimum wage packet (see *Life under Seaga*). As social conditions worsened in Jamaica, Seaga, in his turn, became increasingly unpopular, and, like Manley before him, started arguing with the IMF. In January 1985 the JLP government raised the price of petrol, sparking off a series of strikes and riots. Further austerity policies followed, which gradually revived the popularity of the PNP.

A new phase in Jamaica's political history began in February 1989, when Michael Manley and the PNP again returned to power, ending eight years of JLP rule. Manley promised the US and the Jamaican business class that his new government would be more moderate than the previous PNP regime. It inherited dramatic economic problems, with high unemployment and a record US$3,500 million debt (meaning that each person in Jamaica owes foreign banks and governments US$1,500). The country had also been recently ravaged by Hurricane Gilbert, which had destroyed many homes, schools and hospitals. Since taking office, the PNP government has emphasised its 'moderation' and its willingness to attract US investment. Few of the radical programmes of the 1970s have been resurrected.

Grenada: Revolution Reversed

Grenada was a Caribbean country which attempted an even more radical experiment in development and which consequently met with an even more extreme response from the US. The island is tiny, covering only 133 square miles and having a population of under 100,000 people. When it gained independence in 1974, the country's economy was extremely underdeveloped and almost entirely agricultural. Only 4 per cent of GDP came from manufacturing, while agriculture accounted for nearly all exports. These exports — bananas, cocoa, nutmeg — were controlled by a small class of landowners and TNCs, and tourism, the island's other main activity, was run by a small group of businessmen and their political allies. The divide between rich and poor was huge. A mere 0.5 per

Maurice Bishop congratulates award-winning worker at 'emulation ceremony', 1982

* developing the country's economy by introducing a 'new tourism' which was meant to reduce the role of private owners and foreign interests

In their place, the government itself took charge of some hotels and encouraged local farmers to produce food for the tourist industry. A new international airport was planned for the country, which meant that tourists would be able to fly direct to the island.

Almost at once, life began to improve for the majority of Grenadians. The new government put social development first, and built or modernised schools and clinics. Since many people were involved in this programme and in building the new airport, unemployment dropped from 49 per cent in 1979 to 14 per cent in 1982 and incomes grew. At the same time, the New Jewel government introduced free medical care and a literacy campaign. The government built new houses, too, replacing many of the slums from the Gairy period. In order to protect the living standards of the poor, it strictly controlled the prices of basic foods and other necessities.

cent of the country's farms covered just under half of its farmland, meaning that small farmers were pushed into the least fertile areas of the island.

This unequal society was ruled by the dictatorial Eric Gairy, an ally of the US. In March 1979 a small group of revolutionaries, headed by Maurice Bishop, took power in a popular uprising and ousted Gairy and his corrupt government. Bishop's group, known as the New Jewel Movement (Joint Endeavour for Welfare, Education and Liberation), promised to follow what it described as a 'non-capitalist path'. This included:

* handing over some land from wealthy landowners to poor farmers

* increased government control or nationalisation of certain businesses, alongside the encouragement of the private and cooperative sectors

Although the Grenadian economy remained mixed, the government was nevertheless able to play a large part in planning its development. Recognising the danger of depending upon a few exports (nutmeg, cocoa and bananas) and restricted markets for their exports (the US and Britain), it looked for alternative buyers for the island's agricultural products and encouraged diversification within agriculture (see *Genuine Independence*). It also cut back on expensive imports of food, helping local farmers to produce more food for local

Genuine Independence

For us the most important aspect in building an economically independent country (which is the only way that you can truly say that you are politically independent) is the method of diversification — in all ways, in all aspects. First, diversification of agricultural production, secondly diversification of the markets that we sell these products to, thirdly diversification of the sources of our tourism, the variety of countries from which our tourists come. The maximum of diversification, the minimum of reliance upon one country or a handful of countries means the greater your independence, the less able certain people are to squeeze you, pressurise you and blackmail you.

Bernard Coard, Finance Minister, Grenada, 1979.

March to celebrate the third anniversary of the Grenada revolution

members of the ruling party. Their say in the country's development was vastly expanded through a system of local and workplace councils, and almost everybody benefited from rising living standards and improved social services. Yet the government also knew that the US would not tolerate a system of development which was openly 'non-capitalist' in direction. It encouraged people to join a national militia to defend the island against external attack.

Hand-painted roadside hoarding, 1982

consumption. As a result, the country's economy, which had stagnated for many years, began to expand. In 1982 the World Bank praised the Grenadian economy as one of the few among the underdeveloped nations which was making significant advances.

'The government which came to power in 1979 inherited a deteriorating economy, and is now addressing the task of rehabilitation and of laying better foundations for growth within the framework of a mixed economy...Government objectives are centred on the critical development issues and touch on the country's most promising development areas.'
World Bank Memorandum, 1982

The majority of Grenadians supported the New Jewel government and the leadership of Maurice Bishop although only a small number were actually

What had Grenada done to earn the hostility of the US? Firstly, it was challenging the US view of development by putting the interests of poor people before those of wealthy TNCs. Secondly, it was openly friendly with Cuba, which provided the country with economic aid and technical assistance. Cuban construction workers, for instance, were helping to build the new airport, while Cuban doctors and nurses were training Grenadians for the expanding health service. For the US, this meant that Grenada had become a communist country and that it was likely to threaten US control of the Caribbean. Washington also saw Grenada's open support for other non-capitalist Third World countries such as Nicaragua as a deliberate provocation.

As with Jamaica, the US began to show its opposition by attacking the Grenadian economy. Propaganda against the country was spread throughout the region and in the US, damaging the important tourist trade. President Reagan stopped all US aid to the country. Finally, the US administration began to plan an armed invasion of Grenada. It carried out military exercises in the region to intimidate the Grenadian government, which warned its people that an invasion was imminent.

The pretext for US intervention came in October 1983, when an internal dispute within the New Jewel government led to the murder of Prime Minister Maurice Bishop and other leading members of the government. A faction of the NJM, dominated by the army, took power, but it had already lost the support of most Grenadians. Using the excuse that US students on the island were in danger because of the political unrest, 6,000 US Marines invaded Grenada, easily defeating the militia, and took control of the country (see *The Sledgehammer and the Nutmeg*).

Grenada's experiment in development abruptly ended. This tiny island had dared to challenge the US rule that only one type of social system is allowed in the Caribbean, and due to internal divisions and external force, it paid the price. After a period of occupation a conservative government was elected, keeping Grenada under US control. Washington restored and increased aid, US companies were invited back to the island, and the advances in health, education and housing were reversed. For the foreseeable future, at least, Grenada is destined to be a 'loyal ally' of the US. The much-heralded arrival of US investment, promised by President Reagan, never arrived, however, and Grenada's level of unemployment has again risen steeply due to the closure of state-owned industries and work programmes.

Jamaica and Grenada have both learnt that US governments are unwilling to tolerate development strategies which are not based on the US system and the priority of profits. What these two countries attempted to do was not to destroy capitalism (since both preserved a mixed economy and encouraged private investment), but to increase government control over the economy and to make the economy work for local people rather than the rich few and the TNCs. In this respect, the two experiments worked well. The poor of Jamaica and Grenada enjoyed substantial improvements in their everyday lives, gaining access to health care and education, finding more employment and rights at work, and feeling themselves to have a say in the development of their countries. For brief periods, the two islands experienced forms of development which set out to benefit the majority of people and which actually bettered the conditions of the poor.

Grenada Morning

There was the joy of education, of seeing your children achieving free secondary schooling and your illiterate mother learning how to read and write, the joy of seeing wasted, unemployed youths forming co-operatives and planting the idle land. There was the joy of free health care, of walking to see a doctor or dentist in your local health clinic and knowing that the few dollars you had would stay in your pocket that morning, the joy of going on a Sunday outing and driving in one of your people's own buses along the runway of freedom, a part of the magnificent airport being built in your own small island, the joy of repairing your own house on a Sunday morning with the voluntary labour of your neighbours, using the materials supplied through industrial products, your own mangoes and soursops tinned behind your own labels: 'Made in Grenada', of hearing your own language which your parents and grandparents spoke at your own organs of local democracy that scorned the Westminster imposition and colonial mimicry: all this was the joy that opened the Grenada morning five years ago.

Chris Searle, *In Nobody's Backyard*

Local health clinic established by revolutionary government

The Sledgehammer and the Nutmeg

What can be said about an invasion launched by a nation of 240 million people against one of 110 thousand? And when the invader is, militarily and economically, the most powerful in the world, and the target of its attack is an underdeveloped island of small villages 1,500 miles away, 133 square miles in size, whose main exports are cocoa, nutmeg and bananas...

William Blum, *The CIA: a Forgotten History*.

In many ways, the Grenadian experiment went much further than Jamaica's. Under the New Jewel government, Grenada was a revolutionary society which aimed to break decisively with the past. Michael Manley's PNP government, on the other hand, tried only to reform the existing system to help the poor. What they had in common, however, was a search for social justice and the belief that poverty is not inevitable in the Caribbean.

Both governments also made mistakes. They perhaps underestimated the virulence of US opposition to their development projects and the damage it could do. In Grenada especially, too few people were active in the government party, and the leadership was accused of becoming distant from the majority of Grenadians.

US soldier and local police on patrol in Grenada after the invasion

Trinidad and Tobago: the Oil Bonanza

'Give us this day our daily bread shouldn't be a prayer to Shell Oil'
Third World representative at a conference of the UN Food and Agriculture Organisation

Trinidad's experience has been very different, despite the fact that its oil and gas have earned the country huge sums of money. Before the oil boom of the early 1970s the Trinidadian economy depended largely on agriculture, like others in the Caribbean.

The post-independence ruling party, the People's National Movement (PNM) headed by the historian Eric Williams, also vigorously pursued the 'Puerto Rican' model of development. It introduced the 'Pioneer Status Act' encouraging TNCs to open factories in Trinidad to supply the local markets with manufactured goods. But between 1974 and 1983 the country received a windfall of US$17,000 million in oil revenues, coming mainly from taxes on the

TNCs which were refining and exporting its oil. As the oil boom reached its peak in 1978, the Trinidadian government was receiving as much as 65 per cent of its total income from oil revenues. Much of this money could have been spent on improving its social facilities and developing agriculture. Instead, the government decided to invest in massive industrialisation, believing that this would guarantee the country's long-term economic future. Trinidad now has much heavy industry, based around its oil production, and TNCs are involved in refining and petrochemicals.

A major result of this development strategy is the division between extremely developed areas of the economy — the new Point Lisas heavy industry complex, for instance, — and other areas such as the sister island of Tobago which remain very underdeveloped. The oil wealth is unevenly distributed, favouring some areas and groups and missing out others. Almost twenty years after the oil boom began, 10 per cent of the population still owns 40 per cent of the country's wealth. The poor, in fact, have actually suffered from this type of development, since oil earnings have led to inflation, raising prices sharply (see *The Price of Oil*). Moreover, because the government has neglected agriculture in favour of heavy industry, Trinidad now imports 75 per cent of its food, raising prices for the poor.

Other problems have emerged from Trinidad's oil wealth. The new refineries and factories are poisoning the island's environment. The infrastructure, and especially the road system, is unable to cope with this industrial expansion, largely due to the government's unwillingness to invest in road-building and other communications. Telephones rarely work, water shortages are frequent, and the lack of housing has created slum areas around the major industrial centres, as people use whatever materials they can find to build shacks to live in.

The Price of Oil

**It's outrageous and insane
The crazy prices here in Port of Spain...
Where you ever hear a television costs seven thousand dollars?
Quarter million dollars for a piece of land
A pair of sneakers two hundred dollars
Eighty to ninety thousand dollars for motor cars
At last here in Trinidad we see capitalism gone mad...**

Mighty Sparrow, 'Capitalism Gone Mad'. Calypso song.

Traffic jam in Port of Spain, Trinidad

Haiti: The Poorest of the Poor

The drop in oil prices from 1982 seriously damaged Trinidad's economy with GDP falling each year from 1982 to 1989. The government responded by cutting wages and services and by raising prices still higher. In 1986 a new coalition government was elected in a landslide, replacing the PNM which had ruled continuously since independence. Within months, however, the National Alliance for Reconstruction had split apart over how best to tackle the economic crisis.

For the time being, at least, Trinidad's boom is over and money has stopped flowing so rapidly into the country. While this will perhaps not affect many poor people who gained nothing from the oil boom, it shows the fragility of a development programme which is based upon a single commodity. Trinidad's economy is still highly dependent upon the world oil market. If this collapses and prices fall still further, the value of the island's exports drops accordingly, meaning that less money comes into the economy.

Trinidad's economy, which has depended on windfall earnings and foreign investment, is a good example of how industrial development can damage rather than improve life for the poor. Despite the temporary influx of millions of dollars into the country's economy, the majority of people have gained little, except rising prices and deteriorating social services. If and when the oil finally dries up, it is these people who will be expected to bear the cost through economic austerity policies. The Trinidadian government had the chance to improve everyday life for all its people; instead the rich have become richer and the oil companies have made massive profits.

Haiti occupies the western third of the island of Hispaniola (the remainder belongs to the Dominican Republic) and lies close to the islands of Cuba and Jamaica. It is a different world from both its neighbours, however, in its language, culture and political traditions. Independent in 1804 (the second free state in the Americas after the US itself), it was born out of a 13-year struggle in which the black slaves defeated French colonists and armies from other European powers. It was also 'born in ruins', its once prosperous estates destroyed, its towns burned down, and its people exhausted by war.

The example of the victorious slaves terrified other colonial territories in the region which still depended on slave labour. In retaliation, Haiti was isolated (the US did not recognise its independence until 1862) and lived in fear of foreign attack. Moreover, the French colonial system had left a society where a small minority of brown-skinned,

Toussaint Louverture, former slave and leader of Haiti's independence struggle

Papa Doc

French-speaking people wielded disproportionate political and economic power. The majority of Haitians — black and Creole-speaking — were peasant farmers, working smallholdings on the former plantation lands.

This social divide provoked continual political strife, in which rival individuals and parties fought for power. The instability paralysed the economy, which remained dependent upon coffee exports (to France and the US) and subsistence agriculture. Haiti soon became the poorest country in the region, even though the urban elite grew rich through their control of coffee exports and government finance. The peasantry were at the bottom of the social order, weighed down by high taxes, greedy middlemen and low prices for their crops.

The US invaded and occupied Haiti from 1915 to 1934, in order to protect its regional interests from what it saw as Haiti's chronic instability. After it withdrew its troops, a movement grew up which claimed to represent the black, poor majority. In elections in 1957, a country doctor, named François Duvalier, was elected on the promise of social and economic reforms. Instead, Duvalier, or 'Papa Doc' as he became known, established a family dictatorship that lasted almost 30 years. Under the Duvaliers — Papa Doc was succeeded in 1971 by Jean-Claude or 'Baby Doc' — Haiti became a byword for poverty and repression. The Duvalier family was notorious for its corruption, plundering state coffers and intimidating potential opponents through their private army, the notorious Tontons Macoutes.

Suddenly, in late 1985, Baby Doc's grip on power seemed to weaken. Many Haitians had grown sick of his regime's corruption and the international

scandal of desperate Haitian 'boat people' trying to reach the US. The main supporters of Papa Doc deserted his son, and the army, backed by the US, finally pushed Baby Doc into exile with an estimated US$900 million of embezzled state finances.

As the brief euphoria faded, it became clear that the army, which had taken power, was not going to introduce real change. It promised elections, but when they were held, troops and Tontons Macoutes

US-owned clothing factory in Port-au-Prince

Big Business

Almost all the baseballs used in the United States, including those of the major leagues, now come from Haiti... Haiti has a monopoly not because of any special skill or resources. The monopoly is there because of cheap labour... Tomar Industries, one of several American companies that put baseballs together in Haiti, pays its workers 38 cents for every dozen baseballs sewn. The average girl can sew 3+ to 4 dozen baseballs a day. That's US$1.33 to US$1.52 a day. Baseballs are sewn in Haiti because of desperation...

The sewing of clothing from American textiles is the largest assembly industry in Haiti. Baseballs are next. In third place is the assembly of transformers and other electronic equipment.

Los Angeles Times 8 July 1974

sabotaged them. The generals then imposed a civilian in a rigged election, but he was quickly overthrown in a coup which, in turn, was followed by another change in military government.

While sections of the army have fought among themselves, the majority of Haitians have grown poorer. Under Baby Doc, a number of US TNCs came to Haiti to make clothes and electronics, attracted by extremely low wage rates. Many of these factories have closed due to the unrest, while the tourist trade is completely destroyed. Because of the shortage of good land, moreover, farmers are forced high into the mountains, where they clear the land for food-crops. They cut down trees and sell them for charcoal, causing drastic soil erosion and great environmental damage.

Haiti is an example of extreme under-development, caused by lack of planning, government corruption and dictatorship. It also shows that foreign 'aid' which goes to the government rarely reaches the poor people it is supposed to help. During Baby Doc's period in power, for instance, the US government provided annual financial assistance of up to US$70 million, but much of this money was either stolen or spent on large infrastructural schemes of no use to the poor peasantry.

Yet because the majority of people were excluded from any sort of democratic decision-making, small farmers began to develop alternative ways of helping themselves. They formed cooperatives to press for better prices for their coffee and other crops. Other groups, sometimes with overseas aid from non-governmental organisations like Christian Aid and Oxfam, taught people to read and write, and

encouraged them to share tools and seeds and to work together to stop erosion by planting new trees. Even under the military government, these groups have survived, and some have flourished, since the authorities have not so far seen them as a political threat.

Despite great problems of poverty and political unrest, Haitians are making advances in certain areas because they have decided to act together outside the usual government structures. By working in cooperatives and other self-help groups the poorest people in the Caribbean's poorest country have shown that political parties and governments are not the only channels for change. But until Haiti obtains genuine democracy, change will be limited and poverty will affect most people.

Making decisions

The cases of Jamaica, Grenada, Trinidad and Haiti suggest several fundamental facts about development and the choices which face developing countries:

* planned development, based on changing the share-out of wealth and opportunities in a society, can bring real and significant improvements to the majority of people. Health, education and housing are all areas which can be expanded by increased government investment, while creating jobs and raising living standards.

* development which is mainly aimed at building up industries does not necessarily bring improvements in social conditions and may even worsen conditions for those who are already the poorest.

* even where a country's government is unable or unwilling to bring about any planned development, the poor themselves can find ways of improving their lives outside of central government control.

* Above all, the recent experiences of Jamaica and Grenada have clearly shown that it is very difficult for small nations to challenge foreign interests and control in a worldwide economic system. The power and influence of the US and the transnational corporations are such that experiments in independent development face the threat of interference and disruption. Cuba, for instance, has had to face a continuous US embargo snce the revolution of 1959 which has starved its industry of spare parts and forced it to become dependent on the Soviet Union for trade and aid. The problem is largely one of isolation, since small nations are by themselves extremely vulnerable to economic and even military attack. One possible solution to the Caribbean countries' isolation and weakness may lie in the idea of regional unity.

Eroded
mountainside
in Haiti

Further Reading
Anthony Payne, *Politics in Jamaica*, London, Hurst, 1988.
Tony Thorndike, *Grenada: Politics, Economics and Society*, London, Frances Pinter, 1985.
James Ferguson, *Papa Doc, Baby Doc: Haiti and the Duvaliers*, Oxford, Basil Blackwell, 1988.

Chapter Summary

■ **Jamaica 1972-80 (PNP/Reformist)**

Industrial policy

Parts of sugar, textile, and flour industries and some banks nationalised with compensation. Taxes on bauxite TNCs increased.

Agricultural policy

Some land bought up from TNCs/large landowners and given out to farmers' cooperatives

Foreign policy

Non-aligned, encouraged friendship with Cuba

Results

Short-term improvements in lives of poor, but US and rich elite combine to destabilise economy. Manley forced to go to IMF for loans, who insist on him reversing all reforms.

■ **Grenada 1979-83 (New Jewel/Revolutionary)**

Industrial policy

Some nationalisation, develop tourism by building new airport

Agricultural policy

Expropriate idle land and hand over to poor farmers. Encourage diversification to new markets and crops.

Foreign policy

Strong links to Cuba and other non-capitalist third world governments.

Results

Growing US hostility ends in invasion and reversal of all reforms

---

■ **Trinidad 1974-86 (Capitalist)**

Industrial policy

Government uses revenues from taxes on TNC oil companies to industrialise.

Agricultural policy

Declining sugar industry and food production

Foreign policy

Non-aligned, generally pro-US

Results

Uneven development — some areas of heavy industry, others of backward peasant farmers. Wealth and land unequally distributed. Oil leads to inflation and fall in living standards of the poor, as well as environmental damage. Economy remains vulnerable to drop in oil prices.

■ **Haiti 1957-86 (Dictatorship)**

Industrial policy

Little industry — some US TNCs relying on cheap labour to make textiles, electronic parts and baseballs

Agricultural policy

Very unequal distribution between large rich coffee farmers and small peasants growing food crops.

Foreign policy

Pro-US

Results

Poorest country in the Western Hemisphere

The Duvaliers' Tontons Macoutes, the dictatorship's private army

5. Unity or the Big Stick?

A Divided Region

Centuries of colonial history have fragmented the Caribbean. This fragmentation, originating from the rivalry of competing European powers, means that the individual islands often see themselves as divided by history and language. English, of course, is not the only language which is spoken by people in the Caribbean. There are also countries which speak Spanish, French and Dutch, and most islands also have their own dialect. Individual Caribbean societies, too, are often extremely divided, usually between a rich minority and a poor majority. The colonial experience has left a legacy of racial inequality, sometimes dubbed a 'pigmentocracy', in which those with pale complexions are inevitably to be found at the top of the social and economic ladder. There are also racial divisions in countries like Guyana and Trinidad, where there are large populations of Indian origin.

These divisions have made cooperation between the Caribbean countries difficult, particularly over trade. Each government has tended to pursue its own narrow economic interests, and islands have competed among themselves for trade with foreign countries and businesses, which have been able to play them off against each other. Each island tried to undercut its neighbours, offering lower prices for commodities or better incentives to TNCs. This has weakened the Caribbean's economic situation as a whole, because small and isolated countries are much less powerful than a united group of countries, which together can negotiate better prices for their commodities.

Many politicians and economists have suggested that integration or unity between the Caribbean countries might be the answer to such economic weakness. Countries need not lose their individual identity or independence, but could cooperate in planning their trade and exports. Integration could also increase the region's political importance, since a united group of nations would obviously have more influence than a collection of isolated countries with small populations.

Spanish	
Cuba	9.8m
Dom. Rep.	6.3m
Puerto Rico	3.2m
English	
Jamaica	2.2m
Trinindad & Tobago	1.1m
Guyana	700,000
Barbados	256,000
Bahamas	241,000
Belize	152,000
St Vincent	123,000
St Lucia	119,000
Grenada	110,000
Antigua	77,000
Dutch	
Surinam	376,000
Netherlands Antilles	260,000
French/French Creole	
Haiti	6.1m
Guadeloupe	328,000
Martinique	303,000
St Kitts & Nevis	45,000

The Caribbean's population — and what its people speak

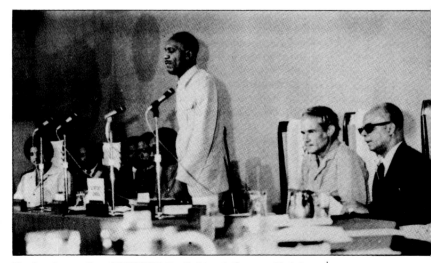

The founding meeting of CARICOM, the Caribbean's Common Market

In order for it to work, integration must be chosen and supported by the participating countries. Sometimes, however, the leaders of the Caribbean countries have refused their support, fearing that integration would endanger their ability to act independently. At the same time, pressures from outside the Caribbean have often worked against regional unity, especially when it has posed a threat to foreign commercial or political interests.

The West Indies Federation

The first attempt at integrating the English-speaking Caribbean territories occurred in 1958, before independence. The plan was developed in London by the British colonial authorities which then controlled the territories. They believed that a federation of ten territories would make British rule and administration easier by creating a centralised system of government.

Understandably, this federal arrangement won little support among the people of the Caribbean. What they wanted was genuine independence and not a new form of colonialism. At the same time, the richer islands such as Jamaica and Trinidad (with their bauxite and oil deposits) feared that they would have to carry the burden of smaller and less developed islands by paying more than them into federal funds. When Jamaica held a referendum in 1961, just before its independence, a majority of its people voted to leave the federation. This marked the end of this particular type of integration, and the federation was abandoned the following year.

Working Together

After independence, the various governments of the English-speaking Caribbean began to reconsider the possibility of cooperating over trade (see *Arguments for Unity*). In 1968, they founded CARIFTA (The Caribbean Free Trade Association) as a sort of Caribbean common market. The participating countries agreed to encourage exports from one state to another by removing tax duties and other restrictions. In theory, this measure was intended to increase the flow of goods between the islands and

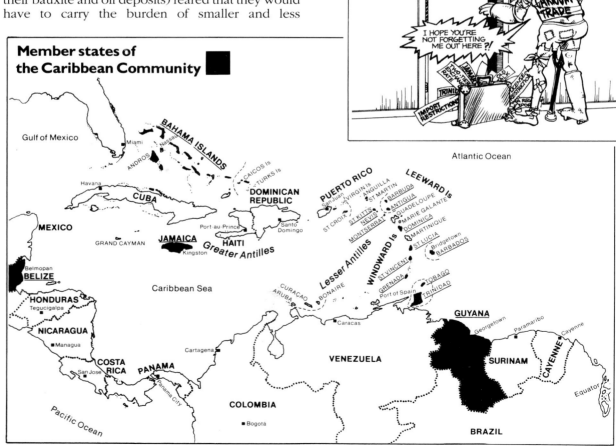

Member states of the Caribbean Community

Arguments for Unity

The real case for unity in Commonwealth Caribbean countries rests on the creation of a more unified front in dealing with the outside world — diplomacy, foreign trade, foreign investment and similar matters. Without such a unified front the territories will continue to be playthings of outside governments and outside investors.

Eric Williams, Prime Minister of Trinidad and Tobago, 1970.

Meaningful independence for the small and very small countries of the English-speaking Caribbean can only be the outcome of political union among these countries — a political union embracing the ten island territories that formed the former West Indies Federation together with the mainland country of Guyana. The essential case for a Union of the West Indies...is rooted in the need to consolidate our sense of West Indian identity and further strengthen our geopolitical situation -surrounded as we are by much larger and more economically powerful countries, both developed and developing.

William Demas, President of Caribbean Development Bank, 1986.

regional market it also set out to create a collective foreign policy for the region and to promote other forms of cooperation. Some of these have been successful. By working together in the fields of education, health and training, the member states have been able to share resources and experience. Institutions such as the University of the West Indies were strengthened by this type of cooperation, and as a result students from the smallest countries (which could not possibly have had a university of their own) were able to study in one of three Caribbean countries. Other positive results have

Campus of the University of the West Indies, Trinidad

been achieved in the area of inter-island transport and shipping.

But despite these successes, many people believe that CARICOM has been an overall failure. In particular, it has never really managed to coordinate what the member countries produce and where they sell their products. Member states often produce the same goods and commodities, creating a local surplus. When they try and sell the excess overseas, the Caribbean countries compete against one another for export markets. In a series of 'beggar-thy-neighbour' policies, each island tries to win markets by undercutting its competitors.

The Caribbean Common Market has failed to weaken the influence of the foreign companies. Instead, the TNCs have taken advantage of a regional market for their products, avoiding the difficulty of dealing with a number of small countries. Some TNCs have also benefited from the CARICOM agreement which removes taxes on certain goods produced or partly produced in the region. By importing materials into the region and assembling or packing them there, the TNCs can claim they are locally produced. As a result, they avoid duty and can sell the products more cheaply and at greater profits, while the state ends up with less revenue to spend on social improvements.

CARICOM has also failed to build a united foreign policy for the Caribbean countries, which would

to reduce dependence upon the US as an export market. In practice, however, the larger and more developed states, such as Jamaica and Trinidad, benefited by selling their industrial products to neighbouring countries, but bought little in return. At the same time, CARIFTA only dealt with trade between the Caribbean nations themselves; it did not attempt to organise the region's trade with the rest of the world. Nor did it include the non-English-speaking territories in the region (whose combined populations far outweigh those of the former British colonies). Nevertheless, the value of inter-regional exports rose from US$85m in 1970 to US$232.8m in 1974.

In 1973, CARIFTA gave birth to CARICOM (The Caribbean Common Market and Community), which was founded by Barbados, Guyana, Jamaica and Trinidad, and later joined by nine other countries. This was a much more ambitious organisation, since besides establishing free trade and an integrated emphasise the region's political independence and common interests. In fact, the opposite has often occurred. Countries have been divided over their attitude towards the US and its regional policies and have disagreed over their relations with Cuba. When the US invaded Grenada in 1983, the CARICOM countries split, some supporting the move and others opposing it.

Despite its faults, CARICOM is nevertheless an organisation which has the potential to work towards more genuine unity and regional development. In order to do so, it would have to win the support of the majority of people in the Caribbean, but a major obstacle is the nationalism which is part of the islands' political traditions. There is also disagreement over including larger countries such as Haiti and the Dominican Republic as full members of CARICOM, which at the moment is made up exclusively of English-speaking nations.

Many new policies and institutions have been suggested to increase Caribbean unity:

* a regional parliament and regional law courts with representatives from all the countries

* a common policy on conditions of work and incomes, which would guarantee basic wage levels and work rights

* freedom of movement for Caribbean people without visas and work permits throughout the area.

Such measures, together with increased cooperation over trade, would certainly make the Caribbean more united and powerful. At present, however, such plans seem a long way off, given the lack of enthusiasm among local politicians.

When integration has been tried, it has often been marked by political division and quarrelling. The most recent attempt at regional cooperation took place in 1981, when seven small islands formed the Organisation of Eastern Caribbean States (OECS). This initiative has not yet produced any real political unity, since the governments involved have been very different in their outlook. A long-term plan is the creation of a single Eastern Caribbean state which would make one nation out of a number of small islands, like the Philippines or Indonesia.

Outside Influence

'The Caribbean region is a vital strategic and commercial artery for the United States. Make no mistake: the well-being and security of our neighbours are in our vital interest.'

President Ronald Reagan

Foreign governments and companies have usually discouraged Caribbean unity, since a divide-and-rule policy makes each island weaker and easier to deal with. Occasionally, however, it has suited foreign powers to bring individual countries together, as was the case with Britain and the West Indies Federation. The US, which is now the dominant foreign power in the Caribbean, has based its regional policy on protecting its investments and maintaining what it defines as stability. To achieve this, in recent years the US has introduced economic and political programmes which aim to approach the Caribbean as a whole (excluding, of course, Cuba) and which aim to direct the region's development along approved US lines.

The Caribbean Basin Recovery Plan (known as the Caribbean Basin Initiative or CBI) was a series of measures introduced by the Reagan administration in 1983. The US claimed the CBI would help the region fight its economic crisis. It includes financial aid to certain countries, tax advantages to US companies which invest in the Caribbean, and duty-free entry into the US market for certain goods which are produced in the region.

But the facts have not matched the promises. Washington chose which countries to help on a completely political basis, and much of the money went not to the Caribbean islands, but to Central American countries such as El Salvador and Guatemala which are included as part of the 'Caribbean Basin'. States the US considered politically undesirable were simply excluded from the plan, while those which conform to US interests were rewarded. In this way, the US turned its Caribbean allies into a dependent group of client states. The CBI plan also bypasses, and thus undermines, CARICOM, which is the official organisation for regional integration.

"You'll love it! Sunshine, good food, dancing, and a chance to observe the Caribbean Basin Initiative at first hand."

The 'Big Stick': Militarisation

'We have stated time and time again that we are concerned about the militarisation of our region, and we want it demilitarised....We do not like this [US] emphasis on the military. Our problems are not military. They are economic and social.'

John Compton, Prime Minister of St Lucia, 1985

Boots Boots

Is it necessary to have so much soldiers in this small country?
Is it necessary to shine soldiers' boots with taxpayers' money?
Unemployment high and the treasury low,
And he buying boots to cover soldiers' toe

I see them boots, boots, boots and more boots
On the feet of the young, trigger-happy recruits
Marching, threatening army troops
Can we afford to feed an army
When so many children naked and hungry?

Lines from a 1980 Calypso song banned in Barbados

The US attempt to bring Caribbean countries into its own 'sphere of influence' does not just stop at using economic aid and investment. The US has also used its military might to dictate the political development of several islands. In the mid 1980s, for instance, there were 21 US military installations within the Caribbean area and approximately 30,000 troops stationed in the region. The largest presence is in the US-controlled territory of Puerto Rico, where there are seven military bases as well as a 12,000-strong National Guard. The purpose of such a massive military presence was made clear during the invasions of Grenada and Panama in 1983 and 1989.

But the US does not simply rely on sending in the marines as a 'big stick' with which to beat governments which differ politically from its own objectives. It is also creating a Caribbean military force capable of stopping any political movements of which it disapproves. To do this, the US provides military training and assistance to several 'friendly' governments (Antigua, Barbados, the Dominican Republic, Jamaica) on the understanding that these countries share the same regional perspective and interests as the US. The smallest islands receive arms and training from the US, while tear gas and riot control equipment are sent to military-dominated police forces.

The Reagan administration used local forces to support US policy when it decided to invade Grenada. Small numbers of troops and police from

US troops in the Dominican Republic, 1965

Barbados, Jamaica, and several smaller states were included in the US invasion force. This gave the impression that it was not simply the US which wanted such a military solution, but the Caribbean as a whole. For any country which wishes to pursue a plan of development which is not approved by the US, the warning is clear. And for those which receive military support, the possibility of independent development is even more remote, since any move in this direction would be seen as an additional threat to 'regional security'.

An example of Haiti's world famous 'naive' painting

The Cultural Invasion

US influence in the Caribbean is not only economic and military, but ideological. One aspect of this involvement is the work of US trade union organisations which try to incorporate Caribbean unions into a regional federation which is pro-US and anti-communist. Bodies such as the American Institute for Free Labour Development (AIFLD) give training and money to local trade unionists who are thought to be 'politically reliable' and they, in turn, lead the Caribbean unions away from radical or independent solutions to the problems of underdevelopment.

Almost everywhere in the Caribbean, people are exposed to ideas and images that come from the US. This process of indoctrination is largely the result of the US media which plays an important part in many people's everyday lives. US radio, for instance, can be heard throughout the region, and the Voice of America (famous for its propaganda) spent US$50 million during the 1980s on setting up eleven additional transmitters within the area. Television is similarly dominated by the US. In 1975, an estimated 82 per cent of programmes seen on Jamaican television were imported from the US. Other Caribbean states had an even more solid diet of US-imported television; Barbados received 97 per cent of its programmes from this source, and St Kitts-Nevis 100 per cent. In countries too small to support a national television service, US cable and satellite stations dominate. Films, videos and news-magazines are also imported from the US. In its campaign against the Cuban government, the Bush administration approved a sum of US$32 million to be used in funding a new TV channel, TV Martí, designed to broadcast US soap operas and anti-communist propaganda to the island

This media invasion increases US influence throughout the Caribbean (see *The Quiet Invasion.* It erodes the cultural independence and separate identity of the various countries in the region and reduces them to passive consumers of news and entertainment provided exclusively by US networks. People in one Caribbean country are likely to know more about events in New York or Washington than about those in neighbouring countries.

However, this process is counteracted to some extent by links between the Caribbean countries themselves. Music (reggae, steelband etc.) and sport (especially cricket) bring the English-speaking islands closer together and often create an identity which is not just national, but regional. This sense of community is reinforced by regional organisations such as the Caribbean Conference of Churches which represents denominations from every country and which organises exchanges and meetings in different territories.

Foreign cultural penetration is also resisted by the Caribbean's own cultural traditions which draw heavily on the historical and ethnic backgrounds of its people. Calypso, for instance, based on the African oral tradition and often a vehicle for satirical political comment, competes strongly with US rock music on local radio stations. Carnival, with its local roots in the experience of slavery, is another powerful form of cultural self-expression. Together with reggae, art forms such as these have become major tourist attractions as well as lasting expressions of cultural identity. In theatre, painting and sculpture, too, there is much activity and regional collaboration, although most local governments lack the resources to encourage artistic development. The advent in 1972 of the regular Caribbean Festival of the Arts, held in differing venues, was an important development.

The Caribbean's cultural strengths are seen most clearly, however, in the writers it has produced. World-class poets include Derek Walcott (St Lucia), Nicolás Guillén (Cuba) and Aimé Césaire (Martinique), while fiction from Alejo Carpentier (Cuba), V.S. Naipaul (Trinidad & Tobago) and George Lamming (Barbados) has become known far beyond the Caribbean. At the same time, scholars and writers such as Walter Rodney (Guyana) and C.L.R. James (Trinidad & Tobago) have made major contributions to political thought. All of these writers, in their different ways, have produced work which is rooted in the particular history and reality of the Caribbean.

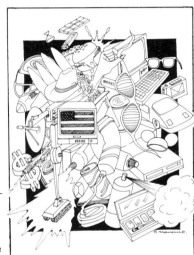

The Quiet Invasion

We all become so immersed in the habits of American culture that if we are not careful we mistake them for life itself. Our habits of dress, our sense of social hierarchy, our acceptance of monarchy can all be laid at the door of British colonialism and the skill with which empire fashions the mind of the governed. But America has never needed to precede its conquests by military action. Hollywood films, glossy magazines, canned television shows have all created a cultural invasion. This has proved more powerful than the attack of any army because its proceeds by stealth to occupy the corners of the mind and needs no fortress upon the ground to uphold its influence.

Michael Manley, *Jamaica: Struggle in the Periphery*

The Case for Integration

There are two main types of regional policy which affect the economic and political development of the Caribbean. One is the type which is imposed from outside by foreign interests. This can take various shapes — cultural indoctrination, the establishment of military alliances, programmes of selective aid and investment. In each case, the purpose is the same: to reinforce the influence and interests of a foreign power within the countries in question. The second is integration, freely chosen by these countries themselves, and free from any outside influence. This sort of regional policy seems more likely to benefit the poor majority of Caribbean people and achieve real development.

Yet in order for regional integration to produce such results in the Caribbean it must go much further than it has gone so far. The first priority for a genuinely integrated Caribbean would be a planned system of trade. The individual states would stop

Carnival in Trinidad

competing among themselves for export markets and instead would work together to obtain the best possible price for their products. Beyond this, integration in trade could also lead to a situation where the various Caribbean states shared an overall plan for production, dividing up agriculture, industry and services such as tourism and banking between them and thus providing a much wider range of goods and services than is currently available. By avoiding inter-state competition, more useful products could be made locally, and these would match local needs rather than foreign profits.

The case for integration and cooperation is a very strong one. Together, the Caribbean nations (and not just the English-speaking ones) could be a substantial economic and political power. This would be a vital step in the region's collective development and would benefit not only governments and businesses, but the great majority of poor people. It is they who have most in common across national boundaries and it is they who have most to win from a properly planned system of Caribbean unity.

Further Reading
Catherine Sunshine, *The Caribbean: Survival, Struggle and Sovereignty*, Washington D.C., EPICA, 1988.

Chapter Summary
■ The Caribbean islands are divided by different languages, cultures and histories, impeding attempts at regional cooperation which could offer a way out of underdevelopment
■ The present Caribbean Common Market, CARICOM, has achieved some successes but failed to end competition between islands for export markets, challenge the influence of the TNCs, or build a united foreign policy. It also only includes English speaking nations.
■ The US is the main outside influence in the Caribbean and has used aid, trade and military force to reward islands it considers friends and punish those which choose a different path to development. Its values are further spread by its cultural dominance in the area, particularly through TV.

Conclusion: Hope for the Future?

The history of the Caribbean shows that 'development' is not always something which improves the lives of ordinary people. There are, of course, different kinds of development, and the Caribbean has been through many of these. Jamaica and Grenada have known short-lived experiments which produced positive results for most of their people. But what the region has experienced most is the type of economic system which serves the interests of foreign governments and businesses and a small, wealthy minority more than those of the majority of local people. From the sugar plantations of the 18th century to the oil refineries of today, the Caribbean has often been dominated by outside powers which have wanted to extract the region's wealth or take advantage of its cheap labour. Its development has been shaped by this one-way process and by the inability or unwillingness of its governments to change the system.

The development of the Caribbean has created and reinforced social inequality. It has produced a tiny, wealthy minority and a large, poor majority. It has created a situation in which the world's most powerful nation treats the region as its 'backyard', attacking any country which fails to conform to its own political designs. It has also put small and isolated countries increasingly at the mercy of an unjust global economic system.

This system is unstable, and suddenly rising oil prices have crippled the already weak economies of some Caribbean states, pushing up unemployment, forcing down living standards, and driving the countries deeper into debt. The collapse in value of traditional export commodities such as sugar has added to the already widespread hardship. As a result, the region remains seriously underdeveloped. Most people suffer from the lack of health-care, education and housing, while hunger continues to blight thousands of lives. Despite the region's resources, the mass of people have grown no richer and have even grown poorer. Only the TNCs and a small number of local businessmen have made profits, and this money has usually disappeared from the Caribbean.

Another form of development is not only possible, but is desperately needed. There are, of course, different opinions as to what this would entail. But many people, both within the Caribbean and outside the region, agree on the most important priorities

Farmers' meeting in Haiti

Carrying water to village from well, Dominican Republic

for the future. In his book, *The Poor and the Powerless*, Clive Thomas, a Guyanese economist and development specialist, has outlined an alternative strategy as follows:

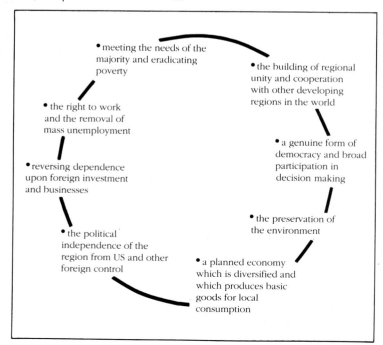

- meeting the needs of the majority and eradicating poverty
- the building of regional unity and cooperation with other developing regions in the world
- the right to work and the removal of mass unemployment
- a genuine form of democracy and broad participation in decision making
- reversing dependence upon foreign investment and businesses
- the preservation of the environment
- the political independence of the region from US and other foreign control
- a planned economy which is diversified and which produces basic goods for local consumption

Thomas admits these objectives could not be achieved in the short term. Nor could they work in a single Caribbean country without similar advances in the rest of the region. Instead, they are basic and long-term goals which should be kept in mind in planning a different type of development. What is needed is the political will on the part of Caribbean governments, working together with shared aims, to build a better future for all their people.

The Poor for a Change

The first priority must be to replace business profits with local needs as the purpose of development. Traditionally, the Caribbean countries have acted as exporters of tropical commodities and importers of basic foods and manufactured goods. This model of development has made the poor poorer by forcing up prices of basic essentials like food (see *Importing Food*).

To change this situation, a government would have to put the needs of its people before those of foreign companies. This would involve putting the most essential goods and services (such as food, clothing, housing and medicines) at the centre of the economy.

Such a change is by no means easy. Many

governments in the Caribbean are reluctant or unable to alter the existing system, and the US would certainly be opposed to any radical change in the region's economic role. Nevertheless there are political parties which are committed to introducing new policies and programmes. And other organisations — local and overseas development agencies, trade unions and neighbourhood committees, church groups and women's organisations — are also trying to introduce an alternative direction in development, not just by winning elections, but through directly involving whole communities and individuals.

Importing Food

Street hawkers sell Washington apples in Haiti, tissue-wrapped pears in Trinidad, and Georgia peanuts in Barbados. Yet it is often difficult to find yams, fresh vegetables, or fresh fish for sale in the street markets of the Caribbean cities. One of the unfortunate trends in Caribbean life is the stagnation of agriculture. Less and less land is under production, fewer people work in agriculture, and more food imports are needed for local consumption. Most of the agricultural production is oriented to exports rather than to providing food for the local market. The Caribbean is a net importer of food: a paradise that can't feed its people.

Tom Barry, Beth Wood, and Deb Preusch, *The Other Side of Paradise: Foreign Control in the Caribbean.*

This direct involvement covers every aspect of people's lives, including the jobs they do, the problems they face in bringing up their families, and their attempts to overcome the barrier of illiteracy. The efforts and impact of these grassroots development initiatives are captured in the following extracts from a recent book by Oxfam, called *Making Our Own Choices.*

Food for export, but basics are imported

Hucksters in Dominica

Roseau, capital of the tiny eastern Caribbean island of Dominica, swarms with activity at the beginning of every week. Bananas and citrus fruit, trucked down from the slopes and upland valleys of the island's agricultural areas are unloaded, counted and packaged in the narrow lanes and streets. By late evening the rickety skiffs and ageing cargo boats in the harbour are deep-laden with crates and boxes of produce. Then aboard comes a procession of women who have spent the afternoon anxiously on the dockside, swearing furiously at every mistake of the loaders and crane operators with the fragile loads. These are the 'hucksters' of Dominica.

Small traders, they brave up to two days journey in these uncertain craft to sell the fruit in the neighbouring islands of Guadeloupe, Antigua, Trinidad and Barbados. Collectively they make a significant contribution to the island's economy.

Dominican hucksters supervise the unloading of produce at Antigua

Cynthia Taylor is a huckster. Most hucksters, like her, are women, often from farming families. Cynthia says 'I have been in my trade over 20 years and I like it. I buy and resell. That's what I'm doing for my living and to raise up my family. I have a large family. My husband is not employed. I can't depend on him for what we need. My husband does gardening. He plants his land. Then I sell what he produces to get what we need'.

The Dominica Hucksters Association, formed in 1981 and led by Cecil Joseph and Dora O'Garo, attempts to provide services and training to the hucksters. Today most of the island's 400 hucksters are members.

The DHA managed to get a few members to keep accounts to see how bad the situation was. Few hucksters carry more than EC$2,000 worth of produce in one trip. The fare alone over to Guadeloupe is EC$200 and the boat owners overcharge for freight. On top of everything else, as much as 30% of the produce was getting damaged by being bruised or crushed in transit. So the hucksters began to see the value of banding together to get improved marketing regulations from the government, to negotiate lower freight costs from shippers, to operate a rotating loan fund. And one very simple concrete step — to use proper cartons (with start-up funding from Oxfam) to reduce damage to the produce. As Cynthia says 'We couldn't deal with these problems as individuals. As a group we are stronger. We can get more attention.'

Sistren Theatre Group, Jamaica

Theatre can be a powerful technique allowing communities to explore their problems. In Jamaica, the Sistren theatre group do just this. Sistren's drama-in-education workshops are aimed at working women.

Sistren, which means 'sisters', began in 1977, when ten unemployed women given temporary work as street cleaners in a government job creation scheme approached a director to help them put on a play. Pauline Crawford, a founder member, explains:

'We were invited to do a piece for the May workers' day. We asked the drama tutor for help in doing a drama piece on how women suffer. We did a piece on the struggle in a garment factory. It was well received. They said "You should stick together". This was the birth of Sistren. We wanted to become more professional. I wanted the play to show what forces caused my mother to treat me like that. This was how "Belly Woman Bangarang" came about. Then we had to deal with the problems of our men at home and our children. You're learning the skills, preparing a production, and at the same time you have to look after your home life. There was a lot of energy among us women, but when you came home it was "why you come home so late? where my dinner?"'

Dominique Lebrun, Literacy Worker, Haiti

Dominique Lebrun was part of the 'Misyon Alpha' team. She explained 'If you don't know how to read and write, you can't participate in local government. People know this is the way they can resolve their health problems, their irrigation problems, their credit problems — in short, their development problems.' In the winter months the sun is already going down by 5.30, when the farmers come in from their fields. There is no electricity in most of the isolated villages. An oil lamp to light a literacy centre would cost almost a third of the year's income for an agricultural labourer, and more than the church can afford to provide. 'But', says Dominique, 'I have seen people come in with their own little alcohol lamps, costing about 30p, lighting the centre with a flicker of many tiny flames.'

The literacy project worked in a multiplier fashion, training a group of 21 'educateurs', who trained 250 'formateurs', who in turn trained about 2,500 'moniteurs' at the base. The dedication of the 'moniteurs' too was tremendous. Themselves poor people who earned only a token payment of around £1.60 a month for their work, they often set out to teach at 4.00 in the afternoon without having eaten a slice of bread all day. They might walk up to five miles to reach the literacy centres where they taught. In the rapidly worsening situation leading to two military coups in 1988, the project was suspended. However many 'moniteurs' are continuing to work as best they can in isolation, training more people in their own areas.

Small and medium scale projects such as these can have an immediate and positive impact on the lives of the people they involve. They may provide individuals and communities with work, an income and skills which would otherwise be difficult to obtain. And because people actively participate in improving their social, economic or cultural conditions, they realise that development is as much about making choices as building roads and factories.

But the positive results of small-scale development must be weighed against the huge obstacles confronting the Caribbean at a national and regional level. Most Caribbean countries face continuing difficulties as the developed western countries turn to other areas of the Third World and the eastern bloc for more profitable investment opportunities. At the same time, the traditional regional exports — sugar, rum, tobacco — are in decreasing demand. Consequently, the Caribbean is trapped between dependency on its outdated agricultural economy and competing with the so-called Pacific Rim as a reservoir of cheap labour. As Europe creates its own single market, moreover, it is possible that Caribbean producers will lose the special and advatageous agreements they enjoy with the former colonial powers for exporting their commodities. This may result in the virtual collapse of the sugar and banana industries after 1992.

The symptoms of the Caribbean's predicament are to be clearly seen in continuing emigration into the US and other territories. They are also to be seen in the growing problem of drugs, both in consumption and smuggling, as an escape from poverty and hopelessness. The region's economic stagnation has also caused massive unemployment in all Caribbean countries which shows little sign of decreasing. Put together, the problems confronting the Caribbean give few grounds for short-term optimism.

Ultimately, it is only governments — and governments working together — which could change the structures and forces which obstruct the Caribbean's development. Until that happens the cycle of poverty and dependency seems set to continue. And for governments to make such changes, they will have to alter the political priorities which lie at the heart of their development strategies. This implies the direct and continual involvement of the people who stand to gain most from a new direction in development. What is required, concludes Clive Thomas, is a conception of this development project which draws on the experience and needs of the majority of Caribbean people:

Moreover, this conception should be elevated to the level of a *popular conception*, rather than simply remaining the possession of the economy's political leadership, technocrats and managers. Rooting the project in the popular culture is the only way of ensuring its success, of organising and promoting the development of a new social order.

Further Reading

Clive Y. Thomas, *The Poor and the Powerless: Economic Policy and Change in the Caribbean*, London, Latin America Bureau, 1988.

Neil MacDonald, *The Caribbean: 'Making Our Own Choices'*, Oxford, Oxfam, 1990.

Sources of Further Information

See page 63 for details about books on the Caribbean published by the Latin America Bureau.

Many of the books listed below are available through bookshops but in case of difficulty contact the publishers.

BOOKS
On the history, geography and economics of the region

The Caribbean — Making our own Choices
Neil MacDonald
An introduction to Oxfam-supported community development work in the Caribbean which firmly locates it in the regional, historical, political and economic context. Interspersed with quotes, songs, sayings and photos.
Published by Oxfam UK, 1990, 56 pages, ISBN 0 855980 86 9
£2.95/US$5.95 (plus 60p/$1.80 p&p) from Oxfam UK

The Caribbean: Survival, Struggle and Sovereignty
Catherine A Sunshine
A comprehensive introduction to the history and present reality of the Caribbean. Themes are illustrated with examples from the English, Spanish, French/Creole and Dutch-speaking territories. Large format, photos throughout.
Published by EPICA, Washington 1988 (updated edition), 255 pages, ISBN 0 918346 07 X US$10.00/£8.00 (plus $1.50/£1.00 p&p) from EPICA and New Beacon Books

The Caribbean Environment
Mark Wilson
Looks at the climate, geology, agriculture, urbanisation and many other aspects of the region. Designed as a textbook but of interest to the general reader. Illustrated with colour photos and diagrams.
Published by Oxford University Press, Oxford 1989, 278 pages, ISBN 0 19 833445 1, £6.95 from Oxford University Press

From Columbus to Castro: The History of the Caribbean 1492-1969
Eric Williams
Painstaking economic history of the region concentrating especially on the colonial period, slavery, and the rise and fall of the sugar economy.
Published by Andre Deutsch, London 1983,
576 pages, ISBN 0 233 97656 6 £7.95 (plus £1.50 p&p) from Andre Deutsch

The Growth of the Modern West Indies
Gordon K Lewis
Historical essays on the English-speaking Caribbean tracing the development of the region from colonialism to political independence.
Published by Monthly Review Press, New York 1968, 512 pages, ISBN 0853 451 303 US$12.00/£7.95 (plus $1.50/ 75p p&p) from Monthly Review Press and Central Books

The Other Side of Paradise: Foreign Control in the Caribbean
Tom Barry, Beth Wood and Deb Preusch
An extensive overview of international corporate investment and its profound impact on the politics and economics of the region. Includes brief profiles of each of the Caribbean islands
Published by Grove Press, New York 1984, 405 pages, ISBN 0 394 62056 9 US$10.00 (plus $1.50 p&p within the USA, $3.00 p&p overseas) from The Resource Center

BOOKS
Country studies

Politics in Jamaica
Anthony J Payne
A study of the island's post-independence history, examining the development strategies of the Michael Manley and Edward Seaga governments.
Published by Hurst & Co, London 1988, 196 pages, ISBN 1 85065 046 2, £6.95/US$29.95-hbk (plus £1.00/$1.50 p&p) from Hurst and Co and St Martins Press, New York

The Hunger Crop: Poverty and the Sugar Industry
Belinda Coote
Third World sugar producers are faced with a shrinking market and ever decreasing prices. Case studies from Oxfam-supported projects (including those in Jamaica) show some of the efforts being made by producers which offer hope in the struggle for survival.
Published by Oxfam UK, 1987, 124 pages, ISBN 0 85598 081 8, £3.50/ US$6.95 (plus 75p/$2.00 p&p) from Oxfam UK

Sweet or Sour?
Neil Larkin & John Widdowson
A study of the operations of the transnational company Tate and Lyle in Britain and Jamaica, focusing on sugar. Large format, interspersed with photos, cartoons, and activities for mixed ability
group work with students in the 14 — 16 age range.
Published by the Association for Curriculum Development, London 1988, 123 pages, ISBN 185401 000 X, £6.95 (incl p&p) from ACD

Grenada: Politics, Economy and Society
Tony Thorndike
A description and evaluation of the economic and social policies of the Grenadian revolution. Detailed information on the 'revo's' successes and failings as well as its final collapse.
Published by Pinter Publishers, London 1985, 206 pages, ISBN 0 86187 415 3, £9.95/US$14.00 (plus £1.50/US$1.50 p&p) from Pinter Publishers

Papa Doc, Baby Doc: Haiti and the Duvaliers
James Ferguson
Explains the reality of Haiti under the Duvaliers and the historical roots and causes of the regime's violent disintegration. Also reconstructs the events surrounding Baby Doc's fall and the subsequent power struggle within 'liberated Haiti', ending in a new dictatorship.
Published by Basil Blackwell, Oxford and New York 1988, 204 pages, ISBN 0 631 16579 7, £8.50/US$9.95 (plus 95p/$1.50 p&p) from Basil Blackwell

The Black Jacobins: Toussaint L'Ouverture and the San Domingo Revolution
C L R James
A 12 year struggle in the Caribbean island of Hispaniola, from 1791 to 1803, resulted in the establishment of the black state of Haiti in 1804. This book is a classic study of that struggle — the only successful slave revolt in history.
Published by Vintage Books, New York 1963, Allison and Busby, London 1980 (first published 1938) 426 pages, ISBN 0 85031 336 8 (A&B) £5.99 (plus 60p p&p) from Allison and Busby

Bitter Sugar
Maurice Lemoine
A powerful documentary (seen through the eyes of a migrant labourer) of the life of Haitian sugar-cane cutters in the Dominican Republic, exploited by the greed of Haitian dictator 'Baby Doc' Duvalier and the Dominican ruling elite, in partnership with US corporations.
Published by Zed Books, London 1985, and Banner Press, Chicago 1985, 308 pages, ISBN 0 86232 446 7 (Zed), £7.95, ISBN 0 916650 18 9, US$ 9.95 (plus 75p/$1.50 p&p) from Zed Books and Banner Press

Sugar and Modern Slavery: A Tale of Two Countries
Roger Plant
Investigations by the author reveal the slave-like conditions under which Haitian /migrant labourers work on the Dominican Republics's sugar plantations. Also includes a study of the modern sugar industry in the Caribbean and the role of the US and its transnational corporations.
Published by Zed Books, London 1987, 176 pages ISBN 0 86232 573 0 £7.95/ US$12.50 (plus 75p/$1.50 p&p) from Zed Books and Humanities Press International

BOOKS
Fiction and poetry

Angel
Merle Collins
The story of a young girl growing up in Grenada, up to and including the US invasion. Centred on three generations of Grenadian women.
Published by The Womens Press, London 1987, ISBN 0 704340 82 8, £4.95 (plus £1.00 p&p) from The Womens Press or through Inland Book Company, Connecticut

Callaloo: Four Writers from Grenada
An anthology which takes its title from the Merle Collins poem which for so many symbolised the struggle and achievement of the revolution. Includes poems by Merle Collins, short stories by Jacob Ross and Renalph Gebon and a short play by Gloria Hamilton. Illustrated by Dan Jones.
Published by Young World Books, London 1984, 108 pages, ISBN 0 905405 09 9, £2.00 (plus 40p p&p) from Young World Books

The Lonely Londoners
Samuel Selvon
Tragi-comic account of Caribbean migration to post-war London
Published by Longman, Harlow 1979, ISBN 0582 642 647 £3.95/US$9.95 (plus 50p/$1.50 p&p) from Longman

Masters of the Dew (Les Gouverneurs de la Rosée)
Jacques Roumain
Classic Haitian story of a peasant community struggling to overcome drought and poverty.
Published by Heinemann, Oxford 1978, ISBN 435 987 453 £4.50 (plus £2.00 p&p) from Heinemann

The Penguin Book of Caribbean Verse
Edited by Paula Burnett
A lively collection of poems illustrating the Caribbean's written and oral tradition. Also includes useful notes and biographies.

Published by Penguin Books, Harmondsworth 1986, 448 pages, ISBN 0 14 058511 7, £6.99 through Penguin Books UK and Viking/Penguin USA

A Small Place
Jamaica Kincaid
A vehement critique of the government of Antigua and its policies. More of a tract than a novel, it reveals much of the venom of small-island politics.
Published by Farrar, Straus and Giroux, New York, and Virago, London 1988, ISBN 0 806068 205 6 (Virago) £3.50 (plus 75p p&p) from Virago

BOOKLETS AND PERIODICALS
Caribbean Contact
Lively coverage of political, economic, social and cultural issues in the whole of the region. Monthly newspaper published by the Caribbean Conference of Churches, Barbados.
Available on annual subscription (US$15.00 for individuals, US$20.00 for organisations)

Caribbean Insight
Monthly economic and political newsletter covering all 35 countries in the Caribbean and Central America. Facts, figures and analysis of economic developments in the region.
Published for the Publications Division of the West India Committee, London, ISSN 0142 4742, available on annual subscription, £56/US$120 (by airmail)

Hurricane: IMF, World Bank, US Aid in the Caribbean
Kathy McAfee
Special issue of NACLA *Report on the Americas* with articles on: the shortcomings of international development aid to the English-speaking Caribbean; Jamaica's 'sellout' to the multilateral banks; Grenada six years after the US invasion; privatization Dominica-style.
Volume XX11 Number 5, February 1990, 40 pages, US$3.50 (plus $1 postage and handling) from NACLA, New York. Details about availability in the UK from Latin America Bureau.

A Mirror to Britain: The Caribbean Community and the UK
A study pack with brief sections on: The Caribbean today; An interlocking history; Immigration 1948-1988; The Caribbean community in the UK today; The challenge to faith. Each section has suggestions for discussion and bible study.
Published by Christian Aid, London 1989, large format, 22 pages plus photo set, £2.95 (plus 50p p&p)

Patterns of Racism
Looks at different patterns of development of racism and colonialism in different part of the world, including the Caribbean and Latin America.
Published by the Institute of Race Relations, London 1982, large format, 44 pages, ISBN 0 85001 024 1, £2.00/US$5.95 (plus 50p/$1.50 p&p) from Institute of Race Relations and Inland Book Co USA

Roots of Racism
Historical overview of European colonisation in the Caribbean and elsewhere and the resulting growth of racist ideology. Illustrated and includes suggestions for work and further reading.
Published by the Institute of Race Relations, London 1982, large format, 28 pages, ISBN 0 85001 023 3, £1.50/ US$5.95 (plus 30p/$1.00 p&p) from Institue of Race Relations and Inland Book Co

AUDIOVISUALS
The Big Wide World
Three 30-minute programmes, made for TV, on Caribbean development. First programme looks at the effect of Trinidad's oil industry on its development and how the protectionist policies of developed countries are frustrating the island's industrial diversification. In the second programme, Grenadian women describe the change brought about by the 1979 'peaceful revolution'. The third programme is a studio discussion about the influence of developed countries on the Caribbean.
Produced by the International Broadcasting Trust, London 1982, Colour, 90 minutes, available on video for hire (£6) within the UK or purchase (£25) from Concord Video and Film Council. Write for details about non-UK hire possibilities

Bitter Cane
Award-winning documentary on Haiti made in the latter years of Jean-Claude Duvalier's regime. Includes interviews with peasants, land-owners and refugees and footage shot clandestinely in Haiti.
Produced by Haiti Films, Haiti 1983, Colour, 75 minutes. Available on 16mm film (£46.00 + VAT for hire) and VHS Video (for hire — £14.95 in advance or £19.55 on invoice, for purchase — £40.00) from The Other Cinema, London and on 16mm film from Cinema Guild, New York.

A History of Racism (ACD)
A film showing how racism in Britain has its roots in Europe's imperial and colonial history. Includes a section on Caribbean history. An illustrated transcript of the text

has also been produced.
Produced by the Association for Curriculum Development, London 1987, colour, 60 minutes. Available for purchase on VHS video (£40) from ACD

Plunder in Paradise
An introduction to political, social and economic issues in the Caribbean, from the colonial past to current conflicts.
Produced by the Resource Center, New Mexico 1984, colour, 25 minutes. Available for purchase as tape-slide or video US$25.00 (plus $5.00 p&p within the USA, plus $7.50 p&p overseas) from The Resource Center

The Treacherous Banana Skin: The Banana Industry and the Windward Islands
Shows the lives of farming families in St Vincent. Covers shipping and marketing of the banana crop and raises issues about their earning power and the future of the Eastern Caribbean banana industry.
Produced by Oxfam UK, 1987, black and white photo exhibition, twelve 20 x 30 inch panels. Available for hire (£10 plus carriage) from Oxfam UK Audiovisual Resources Unit.

Women in Jamaica (working title)
A film on the role of women in development in Jamaica, looking at the effects of debt and structural adjustment.
Produced by Christian Aid, London, colour, 15 minutes, available January 1991 from Christian Aid Films and Publications Unit

ORGANISATIONS

Allison & Busby (publisher), Sekford House, 175-179 St Johns Street, London EC1V 4LL, UK
Andre Deutsch (publisher), 105 Great Russell Street, London WC1B 3LJ, UK
Association for Curriculum Development (resources for education) PO Box 563, London N16 8SD, UK
Banner Press (publisher), PO Box 21195, Midtown Station, New York, NY 10129, USA
Basil Blackwell (publisher),108 Cowley Road,Oxford OX4 1JF,UK
Basil Blackwell Inc., 3 Cambridge Centre, Suite 302, Cambridge, MA 02142, USA
Caribbean Contact (newspaper), PO Box 616, Barbados, West Indies
Caribbean Exchange (aid, campaigns and education), PO Box 146816, San Francisco, CA 94114-6816, USA
Caribbean Insight (newsletter), Commonwealth House, 18 Northumberland Avenue, London WC2N 5RA, UK
Caribbean Labour Solidarity (information and campaigns),

138 Southgate Road, London N1, UK
Central Books (bookshop), 37 Grays Inn Road, London WC1 9PS UK
Christian Aid (aid, education and resources), PO Box 100, London SE1 7RT, UK
Cinema Guild (distributor), 1697 Broadway, New York, NY 10019, USA
Concord Video and Film Council (distributor), 201 Felixstowe Road, Ipswich, Suffolk IP3 9BJ, UK
EPICA — Ecumenical Program on Central America and the Caribbean (information, education and resources), 1470 Irving Street N.W., Washington DC 20010, USA
Heinemann Educational Books (publisher), Halley Court, Jordan Hill, Oxford, OX2 8RJ UK
Heinemann Inc., 361 Hanover Street, Portsmouth, New Hampshire 03801, USA
Humanities Press International Inc (distributor), 171 First Avenue, Atlantic Heights, New Jersey 07716, USA
Hurst and Co (publisher), 38 King Street, London WC2E 8JT UK
Inland Book Company (distributor), PO Box 261, East Haven, Ct 06512, USA
Institute of Race Relations (information and resources), 2 — 6 Leeke Street, Kings Cross Road, London WC1X 9HS, UK
Latin America Bureau (research, information and publications), 1 Amwell Street, London EC1R 1UL, UK
Longman (publisher), Burnt Mill, Harlow, Essex, CM20 2JE, UK
Longman Trade USA, 500 North Dearborn Street, Chicago, Ill 60610, USA
Monthly Review Press (publisher), 122 West 27 Street, New York, NY 10001 USA
NACLA (magazine publisher), 475 Riverside Drive, Suite 454, New York, NY 10115, USA
New Beacon Books (bookshop), 76 Stroud Green Road, London N4 3EN, UK
The Other Cinema (distributor),79 Wardour Street, London W1V 3TH, UK
Oxfam UK (aid, education and resources), 274 Banbury Road, Oxford, OX2 7DZ, UK
Oxfam America, 115 Broadway, Boston, MA 02116, USA
Oxford University Press (publisher), Walton Street, Oxford OX2 6DP, UK
Penguin Books (publisher), Bath Road, Harmondsworth, Middlesex, UK
Pinter Publishers, 25 Floral Street, London WC2E 9DS, UK
The Resource Center (research, information and resources), Box 4506 Albuquerque, NM 87196, USA
St Martins Press (publisher), 175 Fifth Avenue, New York, NY 10010, USA
Tourism Concern (education and campaigns), 8 St Marys Terrace, Ryton, Tyne and Wear, NE40 3AL, UK
Viking/Penguin Inc., 40 West 23rd Street,

New York, NY 10010, USA
Virago (publisher), Orders Dept, Alma Park Industrial Estate, Grantham, UK
Young World Books (publisher) 490 Kingsland Road, London E8 4AE, UK
Washington Office on Haiti (information and education), 110 Maryland Avenue, NE, Room 310, Washington DC 20002, USA
The Women's Press (publisher), 34 Great Sutton Street, London, EC1V 0DX, UK

LATIN AMERICA BUREAU — CARIBBEAN BOOKS

The Poor and the Powerless: Economic Policy and Change in the Caribbean
C Y Thomas
A radical appraisal of the different models of development in the region with five country case studies — Jamaica, Grenada, Guyana, Barbados and Trinidad.
" a comprehensive and informative study ... a work of real interest to a wide range of people."

Third World Quarterly, London

Published 1988, 396 pages, ISBN 0 906156 35 1 (pbk) £9.99, ISBN 0 906156 34 3 (hbk) £29.95 from LAB.
Published in the USA by Monthly Review Press ISBN 7441 (pbk) US$12.00, ISBN 7433 (hbk) US$28.00 from MRP

Green Gold: Bananas and Dependency in the Eastern Caribbean
Robert Thomson
Looks at the history and future prospects

for the banana industry in Dominica, Grenada, St Lucia and St Vincent. Focuses on conditions for the small farmers and includes a detailed study of the company Geest.

" a useful reference for schools, colleges, workers and those wanting more substantial information... written in a popular style that is easy to read."

Caribbean Contact, Barbados

Published 1987, 96 pages, ISBN 0 906156 26 2 (pbk) £4.50/US$7.50, ISBN 0 906156 36 X (hbk) £12.95/US$19.50

Whose Gold? Geest and the Banana Trade

Anne Simpson

A booklet for school students on Geest and the Eastern Caribbean banana industry. Sections include banana growing, the international banana trade, and Geest — the multinational company. Photos, cartoons, interviews and activities throughout.

" the historical reasons why bananas have become the main export commodity from these (the Windward) islands, and not least the fightback here and in the Caribbean, are all imaginatively portrayed in this publication."

Searchlight, London

Published 1988, large format, 32 pages, ISBN 0 906156 28 9, (pbk) £2.50 from LAB only

Grenada: Revolution in Reverse

James Ferguson

The first in-depth analysis of how the US tried, and failed, to turn post-invasion Grenada into a showcase for free-market development. Contrasts the policies of the revolutionary period with the USAID-prescribed programme of privatisation and export-led growth.

Published 1990, 120 pages, ISBN 0 906156

48 3 (pbk) £4.99/US$8.00 ISBN (hbk) 0 906156 49 1 £14.99/US$19.50

Cuba: The Test of Time

Jean Stubbs

"... a highly sympathetic but critical précis of the Cuban revolution after 30 years. By examining consumer issues, human rights, economic rectification, revolutionary ethics and Cuban internationalism, the author goes a long way toward explaining the 'logic' of the Hemisphere's first socialist state. Useful statistics and chronology are an added plus."

NACLA, *Report on the Americas*, New York

Published 1989, 142 pages, ISBN 0 906156 42 4 (pbk) £4.99/US$8.00, ISBN 0 906156 43 2 (hbk) £12.95/US$17.50

Haiti: Family Business

Rod Prince

Considers the historical origins of the 'Duvalier system'. Examines the Haitian economy, the country's social structure and the role of the United States. Written just months before the fall of Jean-Claude Duvalier.

" ..a useful insight into the deep-seated poverty of the tiny state."

New Internationalist, Oxford

Published 1985, 86 pages, ISBN 0 906156 19 X (pbk) £3.99/US$7.00

Under The Eagle: US Intervention in Central America and the Caribbean

Jenny Pearce

From President Monroe to Reagan, examines the history and motivations of US policy in Central America and the Caribbean and assesses its impact on the impoverished people of the region. Over 25,000 copies sold.

Published 1982, 295 pages, ISBN 0 906156 13 0 (pbk) £6.99 from LAB.

Published in the USA by South End Press. US$11.00 pbk (plus $1.50 p&p) from 300 Raritan Center Parkway, PO Box 7816, Edison, NJ 08818-7816.

Forthcoming 1991:

Jamaica: Special Brief (working title)

Hopeton Dunn

Trace the island's turbulent post-independence history, evaluating the records of the Manley and Seaga governments.

To order LAB Books:

For £ sterling orders: please add 20% (maximum £3, orders over £15 are post-free) for surface mail and packing. Orders to Latin America Bureau, 1 Amwell Street, London EC1R 1UL.

For US$ orders, please add $1.50 for postage on the first book and 25 cents for each additional book. Orders to Monthly Review Press 122 West 27th Street, New York NY 1001. Cheques payable to Monthly Review Press